Dear friend,

Don't you wish that you could snap your fingers and guarantee that your children would grow up to love God? Wouldn't it be great if checking certain boxes ensured that our kids would make good choices– the ones that would cause them to be safe and to thrive?

If you've been mothering for a while then you know there's no parenting formula that is failsafe. We have far less control than we'd like. Social media, school shootings, and cell phones that appear to be attached to our children's hands indicate that mothering today is not for the faint of heart.

But there is good news. You have far more influence than you realize. You are also uniquely equipped to pass your faith to your kids. It's time for us to stop resting all our hopes on youth minsters who are young and hip (as wonderful as they are) and claim our authority as mothers. Your unconditional love for your child gives you an edge over every other cultural influence. What you say matters, and your kids are listening far more than you give yourself credit for.

What you hold in your hands is a resource that I pray will kick-start good and meaningful conversations with your daughter. You do not need to have all the answers because Jesus does. May these readings serve as a bridge between your heart and your daughter's, opening the door to subjects that are important to discuss but might not come up naturally in conversation. I pray that the journal prompts would lead to good sharing about what you both think, feel and dream about.

Don't underestimate the power and influence of a mother who fights on her knees for her child, steps into murky conversations with a willingness to listen, and a God who is the ultimate bridge builder and relationship healer.

Praying for you and your precious girl-

Love, Lisa

Lisa Brenninkmeyer
Founder and Chief Purpose Officer, Walking with Purpose

Share your faith with the next generation

Discovering My Purpose is a six-session Bible study designed for girls in their tween/teen years. This Bible study opens girls' eyes to their unique purpose, gifts, and God's love. It includes the BLAZE Spiritual Gifts Inventory, a fabulous tool to help girls discern where God is calling them to be world-changers.

Between You and Me is a 40-day conversation guide for mothers and daughters to read together. Each day compares a lie of our secular culture with the truth found in Scripture. The daily reflection, discussion questions, and prayer prompts will springboard the mother/daughter relationship to a new level of honesty and intimacy.

BLAZE Masterpiece **BLAZE Belong**

- 20-lesson programs designed to help you lead any size group of tween/teen girls to a closer relationship with Christ.
- Both programs include BLAZE Kits, which are full of fun materials and take-home gifts that correspond with each lesson.
- BLAZE gives you the tools to speak to girls about their true identity as beloved daughters of God!

Learn more at walkingwithpurpose.com/blaze

blaze

walking with purpose

SO MUCH MORE THAN A BIBLE STUDY

BLAZE

Between You and Me:

Mother-Daughter Conversations

www.walkingwithpurpose.com

Authored by Lisa Brenninkmeyer and Angelina DeVincenzo

The recommended Bible translations for use in BLAZE and Walking with Purpose studies are: The New American Bible, which is the translation used in the United States for the readings at Mass; The Revised Standard Version, Catholic Edition; and The Jerusalem Bible.

22 23 24 25 / 12 11 10 9 8 7 6 5 4 3

ISBN: 978-1-943173-20-4

BLAZE Between You and Me: *Mother-Daughter Conversations*
(NAB)

Printed in the United States of America

Be who GOD meant you to be and you will set the world on fire.

ST. CATHERINE of SIENA

blaze

TABLE OF CONTENTS

INTRODUCTION

DAYS

DAYS, CONTINUED

APPENDIX

Welcome to BLAZE

Ask any parent today and they will tell you that this young generation is different from all others. Peer pressure has taken on new forms with social media following our children wherever they go. The need to look good, achieve, and constantly keep their image intact can create anxiety, loneliness, and even depression. There has always been pressure, but the way kids today are glued to their phones means that there is never a break from it. It follows them home from school and causes the peer group to feel like their entire reality. The best safety net for this imbalance is to meet these kids where they are and point them to the only one who will love them perfectly and satisfy their need to belong and be valued. And so this is how BLAZE came to be.

BLAZE is the Walking with Purpose program developed for tween/teen–age girls. Our mission in BLAZE is to speak truth into the hearts of girls who are bombarded by lies about their true worth and beauty. Every week, they are introduced to a lie in our culture, which is then countered with a biblical truth. The Bible becomes relevant, and the girls begin to recognize the difference between the loving, affirming voice of their heavenly Father and the voices that tell them they aren't good enough. The young women in BLAZE grow in confidence as they recognize there is nothing they can do to lose God's love. Even when peers hurt them, they know that God's approval is what matters most. They begin to develop an inner strength that changes everything. Teaching these young girls how to use the Bible as a tool for spiritual growth encourages daily prayer and strengthens the bond with God and family.

BLAZE can be implemented in many different ways—in schools during lunch or after hours, in a small group at home, or one-on-one. It's capturing girls' hearts and keeping them engaged in their faith at a time when we often start to lose them.

What you hold in your hands is an adaptation of the BLAZE program into a devotional book format that you can read one-on-one with your daughter. This book provides you with forty days of readings, compiled from the two years of curriculum in the BLAZE program.

Bible Recommendations

What were your thoughts the first time you picked up a Bible? Perhaps you got one as a gift for Confirmation or graduation. Maybe it was a copy you found lying around at home. It could be that the first time you held a Bible was in a classroom setting. Which of these two statements better reflects how you felt in that moment: "I just can't wait to dive into these pages because I know it'll be life-changing" or "This looks boring and inaccessible. I'm sticking it on my shelf"? For most of us, it was the latter.

One of our goals at Walking with Purpose is to teach women how to use the Bible as a practical, accessible tool. There are some obstacles to that happening. One problem is how we approach the Bible. If we open it up to Genesis and start reading through from start to finish, we will likely have trouble understanding what is going on (and we'll probably quit once we get into Leviticus). One of the reasons this method can be confusing is because Scripture is not a book; it's a library. This library is filled with many genres: poetry, letters, historical narrative, and apocalyptic writings. When we don't know what genre we are reading, we can quickly become frustrated. For example, reading Genesis as a science book instead of as inspired poetry will cause us to see faith and science at odds. Far too many people write off Christianity because they feel it can't possibly be true after seeing discrepancies between things proven by science and the way those same things are described in the Bible. This is a consequence of not recognizing the Bible as a *library* of Truth, utilizing many genres of literature to lead us to the heart of God, understand His story, and see our place in the epic tale of redemption. Catholics don't read everything in the Bible literally. We read some things literally, but not everything.

Another obstacle to using the Bible as a practical, accessible tool for spiritual growth is not knowing where to begin. This is exactly why Walking with Purpose has created Bible studies and programs like BLAZE. Being guided through Scripture, being led to the passages that are most applicable to life in the twenty-first century, helps the Bible to come alive.

You may also want to consider Bible tabs as a resource. It takes about thirty minutes to put tabs into a Bible, but it makes it so much easier to find your way around Scripture. You can find Bible tabs at Catholic bookstores or online. Be sure to get the Catholic version, as Protestant versions of the Bible are missing seven books. (At the time of the Reformation, the books of Sirach, Tobit, Wisdom, Judith, 1 and 2 Maccabees, and Baruch, as well as portions of Daniel and Esther, were removed in order to embrace a canon of Scripture that reflected Protestant theological beliefs. Books were never *added* to the Catholic Bible—they have always been there.)

We recommend using either the NABRE (New American Bible, Revised Edition) or the RSVCE (Revised Standard Version, Catholic Edition) translations.

Walking with Purpose™ Website

Please visit our website at www.walkingwithpurpose.com to find additional free content, supplemental materials that complement our Bible studies, as well as a link to our online store for additional Bible studies, DVDs, books, and more!

WWP Scripture Printables of our exclusively designed verse cards that compliment all Bible studies. They are available in various sizes and formats, perfect for lock screens or emailing to a friend.

WWP Playlists of Founder Lisa Brenninkmeyer's favorite music accompany each Bible study.

WWP Videos of all Connect Coffee talks.

WWP Blog for a weekly dose of inspiration and encouragement from our bloggers. Subscribe for updates.

WWP Leadership Development Program

Do you long to see more women touched by the love of Christ, but you aren't sure how you can help? We are here to help you learn the art of creating community. It's easier than you think! God doesn't call the equipped; He equips the called. If you love God and love women, then you have what it takes to make a difference in the lives of people around you. Through our training, you'll be empowered to step out of your comfort zone and experience the rush of serving God with passion and purpose. You are not alone, and you can become a great leader. We offer the encouragement and the tools you need to reach out to a world that desperately needs to experience the love of God.

facebook.com/walkingwithpurpose

twitter.com/walkingwpurpose

instagram.com/walkingwithpurpose_official

youtube.com/walkingwithpurpose_official

pinterest.com/walkingwpurpose

NOTES

Days

NOTES

Day 1

WHO GOD MEANT YOU TO BE

"Unique and different is the next generation of beautiful. You don't have to be like everybody else. In fact, I don't think you should." —Taylor Swift

When God made you, He thought about every detail of your appearance, your personality, your abilities, and your heart. The truth is that not only did God make you—you are His masterpiece! He looks at you and is thrilled with what He has made.

Can you think of a time when you were little and you made something for me? Maybe it was a picture you drew, a craft you made, or a piece of jewelry that you created. I remember so many of those things and I treasured each one. And you were so proud of your creations. But how would you have felt if I critiqued the picture, took the craft project apart and remade it, or stuck the jewelry in a drawer if it wasn't perfect?

I wonder if that is how God feels when you don't see yourself the way He sees you. He looks at you and is so proud of the way He created you. He sees that you aren't perfect—He doesn't expect you to be. You flaws don't make you any less the apple of His eye. No matter what other people have said to you—your coach, kids at school, a teacher, or anyone else—God is completely crazy about you. He loves you. He is on your side. There is nothing that He would not do for you that is for your good.

I want to remind you of that truth, and some other ones as well. Because if you don't start every day with your mind and heart full of the fact that God loves you, you'll spend all your time trying to be like someone else, or trying to earn people's approval, or just trying to measure up.

God doesn't want you to compare yourself to others, and He doesn't want you to try to determine your worth by looking at what other people think of you. He wants you to hear the message loud and clear: You are a masterpiece.

But you aren't meant to be like a pretty picture on the wall. Ephesians 2:10 tells us, "We are God's masterpiece. He has created us anew in Christ Jesus, so we can do the good things he planned for us long ago."

Saint Catherine of Siena said, "Be who God meant you to be and you will set the world on fire." God has good things that He wants you to do, and if His sons and daughters all do their part, we can truly change the world. He wants us to be brave and be who He created us to be—unique, passionate, and gifted. Your unique way of being, seeing, and acting means that you will notice needs that I don't see. You'll see people who need love, and I'll see other people, and if we each do our part, God's love can spread through us to the people who need it. Heart by heart, this is how the world is changed for the better.

Sometimes people think that you can't make much of a difference until you are an adult. I don't believe that for one minute. I think there's nothing more important than the difference you can make in one person's life by offering a smile, a place to sit, a little bit of encouragement. In fact, you can teach adults in your life those very things simply by your example.

In 1 Timothy 4:12, Saint Paul wrote, "Don't let anyone think less of you because you are young. Be an example to all believers in what you say, in the way you live, in your love, your faith, and your purity."

Do you ever feel like what you have to say or what you think isn't valued as much because you are young? That your voice doesn't matter? That isn't true. Your voice does matter. We read that in the Bible, and we can trust what we read in the Bible. If it says it in the pages of the Bible, we can be certain it is true. We'll learn more and more why that matters.

For Discussion

What are some of your unique qualities that you like?

Can you think of anyone God is calling you to love in a more proactive way? Is there a girl who seems lonely? What is something you could do to love her?

What do you think of the truth found in 1 Timothy 4:12, that you shouldn't let anyone look down on you because you are young, but instead you should set an example for others with the way you live and love?

Quiet your heart. . . .

Ask your daughter for something specific that is on her heart—a dream, a worry, a troubled relationship—and pray for that desire or need.

Dear God,
Thank You so much for the time I've had with my beautiful daughter. Help her to believe that You have created her in a unique way, and You love her exactly as she is. Help her to see herself as You see her—as chosen, beloved, and precious. May we both come to know You more and more so that we can live out the challenge given by Saint Catherine of Siena: to be who God meant us to be, so we can set the world on fire!
Amen.

JOURNALING CONVERSATIONS

Sometimes it's easier to share what's on our hearts in writing rather than coming up with the words face-to-face. This section gives both of you the opportunity to write something down, passing the book between each other. It's another tool in your communication toolkit, but it certainly shouldn't replace talking. Each day, there will be a journal prompt. Sometimes the prompt will have to do with that day's lesson; sometimes it's just a fun question that allows you to get to know each other better. You might want to pass this book back and forth, leaving it on each other's nightstands. It's important that what is written here is kept private, so bear that in mind when you choose how the book should exchange hands.

What's unique about you?

MOTHER

My favorite food:

My favorite movie:

My favorite song:

My favorite holiday:

My favorite grade level in school:

I don't like:

I wish:

I love:

DAUGHTER

My favorite food:

My favorite movie:

My favorite song:

My favorite holiday:

My favorite grade level in school:

I don't like:

I wish:

I love:

NOTES

Day 2

TRUTH VS. LIES

From the time Brynn was in elementary school, she had been known as the mean girl. Most of the girls in her class wanted to be friends with her, but not because they were drawn to her kindness or sweetness. The thought of not being in Brynn's "good books" was frankly scary. If she found out someone's secret, she'd use it against the person. Maybe not right away. She'd just let the person know that *she knew something* that would be mortifyingly embarrassing if it got out. She'd keep it in her back pocket until the day it came in handy.

She sniffed out anything that made a person seem different. Uniqueness wasn't something to be celebrated or respected; it was great material for coming out on top by pushing someone down with her words.

She spread rumors, pitted friends against each other, and excluded or rejected anyone who didn't do what she wanted them to do.

This pattern of behavior didn't stop in middle school. She just got smarter and better at manipulating people. In high school, no one dared to challenge her. She was the queen bee, and everyone did their best to be liked by her. Was *Brynn* liked? That didn't really matter. Brynn was in charge of the social scene.

At first glance, you would think a girl like Brynn was mean to the depths of her heart. But it wasn't meanness that was motivating her and causing her to act that way. Brynn was actually scared, insecure, and jealous.

Sarah, the youth minister at Brynn's parish, started spending time with her, and bit by bit, Brynn began to trust her. Feeling safe enough to be honest, Brynn acknowledged that she was miserable. She knew she was mean, and she didn't know how to stop. She asked Sarah to pray that she could figure out why she acted the way she did. So Sarah did that faithfully.

As they spent more time together, it became clear that Brynn had some beliefs that were fueling her insecurity and tempting her to behave as she did.

If I'm not perfect, I'm not worthy of love.
If I'm not in charge, everything will spin out of control.
In the end, everyone leaves.

Here's the thing. Each one of those beliefs was a lie. This was the way that Brynn was *feeling,* but what she was feeling wasn't based on truth.

Lie No. 1: If I'm not perfect, I'm not worthy of love.
The truth? God loves us just as we are. There is nothing we can do to earn His love.

Lie No. 2: If I'm not in charge, everything will spin out of control.
The truth? God is the one in control, and His plan is perfect. It isn't all up to us.

Lie No. 3: In the end, everyone leaves.
The truth? People may leave, but God never does. And because of this, we are never alone.

Here's something interesting: Each of those truths comes straight from the Bible. We can count on what is written in the Bible; we are guaranteed that its words are true.

And Brynn had a choice. She could choose to listen to the lies, or she could choose to focus on the truth. One choice would lead to bondage to habits that were destroying her heart and the hearts of those around her; the other would lead to freedom and joy.

In the Bible, Jesus said, "the truth will set you free" (John 8:32). That's what focusing on truth does. Our hearts are freed as we realize that we are loved, that we are never alone, that God is the one in charge and that we can trust Him because He is good.

I so wish that everything spoken to you was truth, but it isn't. There are a lot of lies spoken *to* you and *around* you. They are lies about your worth, your beauty, your purpose, and your identity.

Archbishop Fulton Sheen said, "The truth is the truth even if no one believes it, and a lie is a lie even if everyone believes it." That means there are some lies that a lot of people believe, but it does not make those lies the truth. And this means that things can get confusing. It can be hard to figure out what is truth and what is a lie.

Do you know how people are trained to recognize counterfeit money? They study the real thing long enough and hard enough that when they see something fake, it jumps out at them. In that same way, we need to focus on truth so that when we hear a lie, something in our hearts says, "Hmmm, that doesn't sound right to me."

That's what we're going to do during our time together. We are going to look at the truth found in Scripture and in our Catholic faith. We're going to learn how to focus on what is true about us and about others, and as a result, we are going to recognize the things that are false. We'll be stronger and happier as a result!

Discussion Questions:

Are there any girls you know who act the way Brynn does in our story? Have you ever been tempted to act like this?

Do any of the lies Brynn was believing (if I'm not perfect, I'm not worthy of love; if I'm not in charge, everything will spin out of control; in the end, everyone leaves) ever cross your mind?

What do you think of the quote from Archbishop Fulton Sheen, "The truth is the truth even if no one believes it, and a lie is a lie even if everyone believes it"? Do you agree with it?

Quiet your heart. . . .

Ask your daughter for something specific that is on her heart—a dream, a worry, a troubled relationship—and pray for that desire or need.

Dear God,

It can be really hard to discern the difference between truth and lies. Help us to draw closer to You so You can help us to understand which is which. May we start to see the difference it makes in embracing truth as You define it. Help [your daughter's name] to be willing to swim against the current. Help her to define her worth by what *You* say about her. Please help her to be a part of a community that creates a culture of kindness instead of competition and comparison. May [your daughter's name] and her friends champion and encourage each other instead of competing. Draw our hearts close together so that we grow in trust of each other. May we know and believe that we are Your beloved daughters.
Amen.

JOURNALING CONVERSATIONS

What is a decision you have made that brought a huge change to your life?

MOTHER

DAUGHTER

Day 3

WHERE THE LYING BEGAN

Earlier, we talked about how important it is to focus on things that are true instead of listening to and believing in lies. But where did the lying begin?

To find the answer to that question, we need to go back to the beginning of the story. The Bible is the story of God's love for His people. You are His beloved daughter, and that means the Bible is your story, too.

It could be that you've been under the impression that religion is a subject at school, something that you have to know a lot about to be good at, something full of right answers and wrong answers and a God who is waiting to catch you making a mistake. The truth is, God adores you, and He wants you to come to Him with your questions and your doubts. Nothing you think or say can scare Him away. He doesn't want you to approach Him like you would a subject at school; He wants a relationship with you. I want you to come to God with your questions, because He truly does have the answers for the things you worry about, and one of the primary ways He talks to you is through His words in the Bible.

There are two parts to the Bible: the Old Testament and the New Testament. Each part is divided into "books," and each book is divided into chapters. These are the big numbers within the books. Within each chapter are verses, and this allows us to find things easily in the Bible—just like an address helps us with the GPS. *[You might want to open your Bible and show her what you are talking about.]*

Hebrews 4:12 tells us, "The word of God is living and active, sharper than any double-edged sword, it penetrates even to dividing soul and spirit, joints and marrow; it judges the thoughts and attitudes of the heart." This means the Bible is unlike any other book you will ever read—it's living and active. It moves into your heart and into mine, and fills us with truth. It's sharper than any double-edged sword, which means it can root truth deep within us with laser-like precision.

The Bible begins with the book of Genesis, and this is the first place where we see the impact of truth versus lies. When Genesis 3 begins, God has created the world, all that's in it, and Adam and Eve. He has given Adam and Eve total freedom. They are allowed to "freely eat of every tree of the garden" except for one. We read in Genesis 2:16, "And the Lord God commanded the man, 'You may freely eat of every tree of the garden; but of the tree of the knowledge of good and evil you shall not eat, for in the day that you eat of it you shall die.'"

So which tree was God talking about? *[Let your daughter answer.]*
[Answer: the tree of the knowledge of good and evil]

What did God say they weren't to do with it?
[Answer: eat from it]

What would happen if they ate from it?
[Answer: they would die]

Eve was in the garden and encountered a serpent. Let's look at Genesis 3:1–3:

> Now the snake was the most cunning of all the wild animals that the LORD God had made. He asked the woman, "Did God really say, 'You shall not eat from any of the trees in the garden'?" The woman answered the snake: "We may eat of the fruit of the trees in the garden; it is only about the tree in the middle of the garden that God said, 'You shall not eat it or even touch it, or else you will die.'"

This is where we first see Satan in the Bible, and his very first action is to question what God said. "Did God *really* say . . . ?" He planted a seed of doubt in Eve's mind.

Let's take a look at Eve's words. Do you see anything strange? Anything that doesn't match up with something we read earlier? Look back at Genesis 2:16. What difference do you find?

> And the Lord God commanded the man, "You may freely eat of every tree of the garden; but of the tree of the knowledge of good and evil you shall not eat, for in the day that you eat of it you shall die."

What's the difference? Eve added to God's words.

God hadn't said that she couldn't *touch* the fruit, just that she couldn't *eat* it. As she talked to the serpent, she started to get a little fuzzy on the facts. And how did the serpent reply? We find out in Genesis 3:4–5.

> But the snake said to the woman: "You certainly will not die! God knows well that when you eat of it your eyes will be opened and you will be like gods, who know good and evil."

Or in other words, "You won't die. There won't be consequences for your actions. At least not bad ones. In fact, you'll become smarter. You'll be like God."

And Eve had a choice. Who was she going to listen to? God or the serpent?

Let's look at how Jesus describes the serpent (the devil) in John 8:44: "He was a murderer from the beginning, not holding to the truth, for there is no truth in him. When he lies, he speaks his native language, for he is a liar and the father of lies."

Eve's choice was to listen to the lie or listen to the truth. And we have the same choice in front of us.

Sometimes we don't know what to do because we're scared or because we don't know what's true. And that's where the Bible comes in. The Bible is the best source of truth, and the more we know what is in this book, the more we'll be able to recognize what's a lie and what is true.

This is what we're going to explore together. Each day, we're going to start looking at the lies that swirl around us, and then explore the Bible for the truths we can grab hold of instead.

In 2 Corinthians 10:5 we're told to "Take every thought captive to Christ." The way to do this is to take a thought, something someone has said, or something you have read and hold it up. Look at it. Don't just automatically believe it. Ask yourself, "Is it true? Is it consistent with what we read in the Bible?" If it's not, if it's actually a lie, then throw it away, and replace it with a truth found in Scripture. We'll learn more about how to do this as time goes on, so don't worry if that sounds confusing or doesn't make sense right now. It will in time.

But in the meantime, I encourage you to start praying every day, asking God to help you recognize what is truth and what is a lie. That's a prayer He is very happy to answer.

Discussion Questions:

Have you ever thought of the Bible as a place where you can find answers to your questions? Are you ever afraid to bring your questions to God?

Where do you usually go with your questions?

What do you think it means to "Take every thought captive to Christ"?

Quiet your heart. . . .

Ask your daughter for something specific that is on her heart—a dream, a worry, a troubled relationship—and pray for that desire or need.

Dear God,
I pray that Your Word, the Bible, will come alive in my daughter's life. I pray that the truths in the Bible would be lodged in my daughter's heart with laser-like precision. There are so many lies that swirl around us—lies that tell us we need to get all A's to be good enough, lies that tell us our bodies need to look a certain way in order to be beautiful, lies that tell us that our worth depends on how athletic we are. The Bible says something different. Please open up my daughter's heart so she can start to embrace your truth and reject the lies.
Amen.

JOURNALING CONVERSATIONS

Would you rather revisit a day in your past or spend a day in the future? What kind of a day would you want it to be?

MOTHER

DAUGHTER

NOTES

Day 4

SELF-WORTH

Some days go just the way we would have hoped. And then there are those days that make us wish we had stayed in bed. Maybe it's because of things that have been said about us or to us, maybe it's because we failed at something that mattered to us, or it can just be an overall feeling that we aren't worth much.

The truth is, no matter what happens on a given day, you remain dearly loved. God has declared that you are worth everything to Him.

> The story is told of a girl named Sarah. She was sixteen years old and the adventure of the day beckoned her to come, enjoy, explore! She was supposed to go to school, but Sarah spent the day in the rugged and stunning mountains instead. It had been a glorious day. Driving home in the early evening Sarah's thoughts wandered. She felt so at home in the mountains, so refreshed. Suddenly, a car flashed into Sarah's view as it ran a red light and struck her car head on.
>
> The force of the impact sent Sarah, who was not wearing a seat belt, crashing headfirst through the windshield. As she flew through the air, her left knee caught her, and then thrust her back through the broken glass into the smashed front seat of her car.
>
> Badly hurt and bleeding profusely, Sarah's stunned mind took a while to kick into gear. Her first thoughts were, I deserved this. If I hadn't skipped school, this never would have happened. Wounded and bleeding, she believed it was her fault.
>
> As fate would have it, Sarah's next door neighbor was in the car behind her and witnessed the whole accident. Using her cell phone, she called Sarah's parents as they were getting ready for dinner. "You'd better come down here. Sarah's been in an accident," she told Sarah's father. The neighbor's calmness led Sarah's dad to imagine a mere fender bender, and so with irritation and no rush, he drove to the intersection to help with the insurance paperwork.

The situation he had anticipated was not the one he arrived to find.

When Sarah's father pulled up to the intersection, he found police cars, fire trucks, and ambulances. He saw the smashed car of the other driver . . . and he saw his daughter's car, utterly demolished. Walking toward it with fear, he could see Sarah in the front seat. Sarah could see him as well and she began to yell out, "Daddy, it's not my fault! Daddy, it's not my fault!"

"I can see that!" he assured. What he could also see were the firefighters trying to use the Jaws of life to remove the door from the car so they could extricate Sarah from the tangled metal, but the hydraulic tools weren't working. Precious minutes passed. The Jaws of Life were literally not cutting it.

So Sarah's father took action. With **fierce passion and love for his daughter**, he pushed the firefighters aside, and with his bare hands he ripped the door from the car.

True story.

In that moment, Sarah's father forever answered her question of whether or not she was loved by him. Did he delight in her? Would he protect her, fight for her? Was she worth it? Yes, yes, and forever yes."[1]

To your question, "What am I worth to God?" Jesus answers, "Everything."

Just as Sarah was trapped in her car, we are trapped in the snare of sin. We can't get out on our own. God knew that even with our best efforts at holiness, we still weren't going to be able to pull ourselves out of the mess that sin has created in our world and in our hearts.

So what did God do? He decided to send a prince to rescue us. This Prince of Peace came to pull us out of our devastating state of sin, to give us a fresh start, and to forgive us. He came to fix what was broken in our relationship with God.

Rescuing you was worth everything to Him. What did it cost Jesus to rescue you? How much does He love you? To answer this question, we don't look at our circumstances. We look at the cross.

---

[1] Stasi Eldredge, *Your Captivating Heart* (Nashville, TN: Thomas Nelson, 2007), 69–72.

When Jesus was mocked and scorned by the religious leaders, He thought, "You, my beloved daughter, are worth it." When His flesh was ripped from His back as He was flogged, He knew your rescue was worth that price. When He carried His cross on His bleeding back, thoughts of you kept Him going. When He hung on the cross, every breath filled with excruciating pain, knowing that He only needed to say a word and angels would come and rescue Him, thoughts of you helped Him persevere.

He loved you so much that no pain, no scorn, not even death distracted Him from the purpose of fighting for you. Your whole life He has been telling you how He loves you.

Saint Teresa of Calcutta said that for love to be real, it has to cost something. True love is sacrificial. It has to empty us of self. We've felt that to be true in our own lives. Which of these two gifts feels more like one given in love—one that was saved up and sacrificed for, or one that is regifted, costing the giver nothing? But just to clarify, this doesn't mean that we stay in relationships that aren't healthy because that's the "cost." It doesn't mean that we give to others whatever they ask for—and this is especially important in your relationships with boys. It doesn't mean that a girl gets to bully you and make you do whatever she wants. I am talking about the way *God* loves us.

Real love comes at a cost, and nowhere is that more true than with God and His love for us. Open your Bible to Romans 5:8 and read along with me: "God shows his love for us in this—that while we were still sinners, Jesus died for us." Underline that verse. Jesus didn't wait until we were perfect. He died for us while we were still sinners, messed up and needing help.

Because it is so critical that we understand this truth, this is something that the devil loves to lie about. He lies and tells us that God only loves us when we're perfect. Or that if we mess up, God loves us a little bit less. He tells us that we're not worth fighting for. None of those things are true. What is the truth? God's love doesn't ever fade or change. It stays the same—strong and steadfast—no matter what we do. His love can be counted on. He loves you so much that He died for you. He not only has said, He has *shown* that you are worth fighting for.

Discussion Questions:

Have you ever wondered if you are worth fighting for?

Have you ever felt that God's love for you weakens when you make a mistake?

When have you experienced someone loving you sacrificially?

Quiet your heart. . . .

Ask your daughter for something specific that is on her heart—a dream, a worry, a troubled relationship—and pray for that desire or need.

Dear God,
May [your daughter's name] know and believe that she is worth fighting for. You see her and her true beauty, and love her simply because she belongs to You. Help her to believe that she is worthy of respect, kindness, and love. Help her to know that there isn't a moment in the day when she is alone or ignored. You are always by her side.
Amen.

JOURNALING CONVERSATIONS

What do you wish you could change about yourself?

MOTHER

DAUGHTER

NOTES

Day 5

TRUE BEAUTY

We get messages all the time that tell us what it means to be beautiful. We hear that we need to be thin or athletic, or look amazing in a bikini, or know how to create the perfect cat eye. The list of requirements seems never-ending, and the messages don't stop even when we get older.

Probably no one feels this pressure more than the celebrities we follow. Selena Gomez is no stranger to these messages, and this is what she has to say in response: "I realize everybody wants what they don't have. But at the end of the day, what you have inside is much more beautiful than what's on the outside!" We'll be so much happier if we can look at ourselves through that lens.

In order to get the right perspective on beauty, we need to go back to the very beginning of creation. When God created man, He "saw all that he had made, and it was very good" (Genesis 1:31). Do you know what that means? It means that God gets to define beauty because He created it.

What in this room did God make? While He made a lot of the original materials in this room—He made the trees, which have given us wood, which gave us furniture and so on—the only things that were made entirely by God are the people. Do you know that when God looks at us, He says the same thing He said at creation: "This is very good"? He looks at you, smiles, and says, "She is *good*." Let that truth soak into your heart. Our culture has hijacked the definition of beauty and twisted it into something purely external, but that doesn't change its true definition. Who gets to define true beauty? *God.* Why? *He created it.*

God wants us to regard our bodies as good. Even as we read that sentence, most of us start to think about all the aspects of our bodies that we *don't* think are good. This is because we dissect our body parts, measuring each one against the cultural ideal. And this is messed-up thinking. This is not the way God wants us to analyze our bodies' worth. He wants our focus to be renewed and for us to see that He's given each one of us a body not so that we can gain attention or admiration, but so that we can love and serve.

There's a story I want to share with you from the Bible, and it's about a group of men. You might think it isn't relevant for a tween/teen girl, but just wait. There's a really important message at the end.

God's people, the Israelites, wanted to have a king like all the other nations around them. God had been ruling and guiding them, but they compared themselves to others, and they didn't want to be different. God told Samuel, who was a prophet (someone God speaks through), that He would show him who should be anointed as the next king.

God told Samuel to go to a man named Jesse and to take a look at his sons. One of them was going to be God's choice. This was good news for Jesse, so he lined them up. Samuel looked at the handsome ones, the strong ones, the obviously capable ones, and each time, God said, "No. This isn't the one." Seven sons passed in front of Samuel.

This didn't make any sense to Samuel. He thought they looked like the perfect pick, but God said to him, "Do not look at his appearance or his physical stature, because I have refused him. For the Lord does not see as man sees, for man looks at the outward appearance, but the Lord looks at the heart" (1 Samuel 16:7).

Samuel asked Jesse if he had any more sons, and Jesse said the only one left wasn't particularly impressive—he was out in the pasture, looking after the sheep. When that son, David, was brought in, God told Samuel, "He's the one." And David was anointed the next King of Israel.

What God said about Jesse's sons is what He still says today. He encourages us to not look at the outside appearance. True beauty is found inside. It's found in the heart. You have a beauty to share.

I know it's hard to see that. Everyone struggles with it—even celebrities like Taylor Swift. She has been quoted as saying, "I definitely have body issues, but everybody does. When you come to the realization that everybody does—even the people I consider flawless—you can start to live with the way you are."

But I want you to do more than just live with the way you are. You have something beautiful within to offer the world. You are God's precious daughter. He wants you to feel confident and beautiful, not because you're having a good hair day or your face is clear. He wants you to give your heart more focus than you do your appearance.

Our lie for today is this: What matters most is what I look like. The truth? We find it in the Bible in 1 Samuel 16:7: "For the Lord does not see as man sees, for man looks at the outward appearance, but the Lord looks at the heart."

You are beautiful because God created you and dwells in you. That's what gives you dignity, worth, and beauty.

We're going to keep talking about true beauty. It's all about the state of our hearts. What's in our hearts ends up coming out in the way we talk to and treat others. But for now, for today, I want you to start looking at yourself in the mirror a little differently. Instead of looking at your face and body and critiquing, I want you to recite Psalm 139:14: "I am fearfully and wonderfully made." Why? Because you are. And God does not make mistakes.

Discussion Questions:

What are some of the places where you get messages about how important it is to be beautiful?

How do those messages make you feel?

Do you spend more time focusing on what our culture tells you is beautiful or what God says is beautiful?

Quiet your heart. . . .

Ask your daughter for something specific that is on her heart—a dream, a worry, a troubled relationship—and pray for that desire or need.

Dear God,
Please help [your daughter's name] to see and believe that she is fearfully and wonderfully made. May she start to rethink the way beauty is defined, choosing to see it through Your eyes. May she have the humility to acknowledge that You, as the creator of beauty, have the right to define it. And You define beauty as what goes on inside. Help her to grow increasingly beautiful in the ways that matter—in her inner life, in her heart.
Amen.

JOURNALING CONVERSATIONS

My favorite thing about you is . . .

MOTHER

DAUGHTER

Day 6

BEAUTY IN THOUGHT

A few years ago in England, a great commercial ran for the *Independent* newspaper. In the ad, the camera focused on an old woman walking down a street with brownstone apartment buildings in the background. Suddenly from the left, a wild-looking kid ran toward her and tackled her, and the two of them flew a couple of feet on the ground. The film froze, leaving the viewer to shake his head over another example of violence among our youth. Then the camera panned out, and we saw the same scene again. This time, we were able to view what was going on above the head of the old woman. Movers were hoisting a grand piano up on a pulley and platform to move it through a window of the apartment building, and the piano began to fall. It was at this point that the wild-looking kid ran toward the older woman, knocking her out of the way and saving her life. The caption read: "Some papers tell you what you want to hear; we give you the whole picture."

How often do we hear only what we want to hear, without seeing the whole picture? Have you ever heard someone talking about another girl, and instead of making sure that all the facts were right, you believed what you heard? Almost always, we are missing the whole picture. We are always at least one fact short of a full understanding of what is going on. Do you think we would treat each other differently if all our hurts, the wounds in our hearts, were visible on the outside?

But that's not how life works, and all too often, we fill in the gaps and think we have the whole picture. President John F. Kennedy touched on this when he said, "Too often we . . . enjoy the comfort of opinion without the discomfort of thought."

We often make the mistake of assuming "thinking" is something that just happens—something that goes on in our heads that we can't help. Because of this, many of us believe the lie that what we think about doesn't matter.

The Bible tells us something different. The truth is found in 2 Corinthians 10:5, where we're told to "take every thought captive to Christ."

This means that we shouldn't just let thoughts run wild in our heads. Instead we are to take each thought, hold it up, look at it, and run it through two tests. This is especially important to do when we get stuck in a rut—when we're mad at someone and can't stop thinking about it, when we're worried about something and can't stop thinking about it, or when we're afraid of something and can't stop thinking about it.

What's the first test? We hold up the thought and compare it to the truth we find in Scripture. If the thought is consistent with truth, then we keep it. But if it isn't, we reject it, throw it out.

Here is an example of a thought that might flit through your head: "I can't change my bad habits."

What's the first test? We are to ask: "Is it true?"

The Bible tells us that this thought, "I can't change my bad habits," isn't true, because in Philippians 4:13 we read, "I can do all things through Christ who strengthens me."

This means the thought gets rejected.

How about this thought? "My physical appearance is the measure of my beauty." The Bible tells us that thought isn't true, because in 1 Samuel 16:7 we read, "For man looks at the outward appearance, but the Lord looks at the heart."

Here's another thought that can mess with our hearts: "I'm not worth fighting for." The Bible tells us that's a lie, because we read in Romans 5:8, "While we were still sinners, Christ died for us."

So we hold up the thought and compare it to the truth that we know from God. This shows us why it's important that we know how to distinguish truth from lies, and know that the source of truth is God and His words.

Does that mean that every *true* thought we have should be dwelled on? No. This brings us to the second test. The Bible tells us the types of thoughts we're supposed to focus on. Saint Paul lays it out for us in Philippians 4:8: "Whatever is true, whatever is noble, whatever is right, whatever is pure, whatever is lovely, whatever is admirable—if anything is excellent or praiseworthy—think about such things."

So when you have a thought, run it through the THINK test. Is it:
True?
Helpful?
Inspiring?
Necessary?
Kind?

Let's try to THINK in the way that God wants us to—focusing on whatever is true, whatever is noble, whatever is right, whatever is pure, whatever is lovely, whatever is admirable, excellent, or praiseworthy.

Discussion Questions:

Have you ever heard gossip about you or another person that later turned out to be untrue?

If you heard girls gossiping at school, what is something you could say to check the facts?

Do any thoughts pop into your head that you think might be different from what God says is true about you? Can you identify any lies you hear that sometimes sound believable?

Quiet your heart. . . .

Ask your daughter for something specific that is on her heart—a dream, a worry, a troubled relationship—and pray for that desire or need.

Dear God,
Please help us to have the humility to recognize that we don't have the whole picture of what is really going on in another person's life. May this help us to be kinder in the way that we think about others. When we start to get hurt, angry, or offended, help us to quietly say to ourselves, "There is probably more to this than meets the eye." Before we speak, may we think, "Is it true? Is it helpful? Is it inspiring? Is it kind?" If it isn't, help us to not say it, and help us to replace the negative thoughts with something positive.
Amen.

JOURNALING CONVERSATIONS

For mom: What was the hardest part of going to school when you were your daughter's age? What was the best part?

For daughter: What is the hardest part of going to school? What is the best part?

MOTHER

DAUGHTER

Day 7

BEAUTY IN SPEECH

Our words have tremendous power for good or for harm. Someone who knew that well was a girl named Mary Ann Bird. In her story, "The Whisper Test," we see the impact that a few kind words can make.

> [Mary Ann] was born with multiple birth defects: deaf in one ear, a cleft palate, a disfigured face, crooked nose, lopsided feet. As a child, Mary Ann suffered not only the physical impairments but also the emotional damage inflicted by other children. "Oh Mary Ann," her classmates would say, "What happened to your lip?"
>
> "I cut it on a piece of glass," she would lie.
>
> One of the worst experiences at school, she reported, was the day of the annual hearing test. The teacher would call each child to her desk, and the child would cover first one ear, and then the other. The teacher would whisper something to the child like "the sky is blue" or "you have new shoes." This was "the whisper test." If the teacher's phrase was heard and repeated, the child passed the test. To avoid the humiliation of failure, Mary Ann would always cheat on the test, secretly cupping her hand over her one good ear so that she could still hear what the teacher said.
>
> One year Mary Ann was in the class of Miss Leonard, one of the most beloved teachers in the school. Every student, including Mary Ann, wanted to be noticed by her, wanted to be her pet. Then came the day of the dreaded hearing test. When her turn came, Mary Ann was called to the teacher's desk. As Mary Ann cupped her hand over her good ear, Miss Leonard leaned forward to whisper. "I waited for those words," Mary Ann wrote, "which God must have put into her mouth, those seven words which changed my life." Miss Leonard did not say, "The sky is blue" or "You have new shoes." What she whispered was "I wish

you were my little girl." Mary Ann went on to become a teacher herself, a person of inner beauty and great kindness.[2]

Saint Teresa of Calcutta said, "Kind words can be short and easy to speak, but their echoes are truly endless." Words that have a huge impact aren't just those spoken by adults. The things that you say to kids at school and to your siblings are equally important. All the words we speak, all the messages we give are shot like arrows into other people's hearts. They can pierce a heart and make it feel loved, or they can truly do lasting damage.

Sometimes it's easy to speak words of kindness, but other times it can be really hard. When someone is getting bullied in school, we can usually point out the bully pretty easily. "It's him," or "It's her," we'll say, and gesture toward the person who has said something mean. What we forget is that what allows a bully to exist *isn't* the bully's ability to create new mean things to say.

One of the lies I want to talk about to you is this: "The bully is the one who says and does mean things." Do you know the truth? What allows him or her to exist is all the people around him or her who *don't say anything*—the ones who silently watch someone being made fun of or hurt. The people who see what is wrong but are afraid to stand up and defend the person being bullied are actually playing a significant part in the bullying.

We all know why people stay silent. When we speak up, we risk being the recipient of the next round of bullying. But silence at those times is not right. Protecting ourselves instead of the person being hurt is not the right choice.

We are called to speak the truth, even if our voices shake.

You can be brave in this way. You have powerful words inside you, and you can use them to defend the defenseless, to build up the person who is discouraged, and to say something kind to the person who is just plain awkward.

How do you use your words—to defend yourself, or to stand up for those who are defenseless?

Your words have tremendous power for good or ill. Ephesians 4:29 tells us, "Do not let any unwholesome talk come out of your mouths, but only what is helpful for building others up according to their needs, that it may benefit those who listen."

---

[2] Thomas G. Long, *The Witness of Preaching* (Louisville, KY: Westminster John Knox Press, 2005), 212.

This is another area of life where there's a lot of lying going on. One of the most powerful lies is: I can't help what I say. When we believe this lie, we make excuses like, "It just came out of my mouth," or "I wasn't thinking," or "I couldn't help it."

The truth is, God never asks us to do something that He doesn't give us the power to accomplish. If He asks us to be careful with our words, then we can trust that He will help us by giving us self-control when it comes to our mouths. But we have to ask for that help. We do that through prayer.

What a difference it would make if you decided that you would not stand for bullying and unkind words being spoken in your presence. *Everything* might change if you decided to use your words for good, to build others up.

So that is my challenge and my prayer for you. Use your beautiful voice. Speak the truth, speak kindness, speak encouragement. Be constantly on the lookout for the farthest person out, for the person sitting alone, for the person no one seems to like. Speak kindly and watch the ripples spread. Use your words for good.

Discussion Questions:

How have you experienced bullying?

What are your thoughts about the impact that bystanders' silence has on bullying?

Is there an area of your life where you feel God is calling you to speak the truth even if your voice shakes?

Quiet your heart. . . .

Ask your daughter for something specific that is on her heart—a dream, a worry, a troubled relationship—and pray for that desire or need.

Dear God,
Help us to know that You never require anything of us that You don't also equip us to do. It's a lie to say that we can't help what we say. *You* are always willing to help us speak with kindness and carefulness. We echo the words of Psalm 141:3, which asks You to set a guard over our mouths, Lord, and keep watch over the door of our lips.

May we only let out words that build others up and encourage them. May we look for the farthest person out and offer him or her life-giving words.
Amen.

JOURNALING CONVERSATIONS

What is something that is causing you to worry?

MOTHER

DAUGHTER

NOTES

Day 8

LOVED BY THE FATHER

Each one of us was created with a God-shaped vacuum inside. This is a place in our hearts that was made for God. Saint Augustine said, "Our hearts are restless until they rest in you." But God is a gentleman. He knows that until *He* fills that emptiness, we won't be happy, but He waits to be invited in. But the only way we are going to want God to be close to us is if we believe that He loves us. Otherwise, we'll always keep Him at a safe distance.

Many things get in the way of our really believing that God loves us. We tend to attribute to God the characteristics of our dads. If our dads don't express love very well, we might find it hard to believe that our heavenly Father loves us unconditionally.

Sometimes things happen in our lives that we don't understand—things that are really, really hard. Suffering can make it hard to believe that God really loves us—if He does, then why does He allow certain hardships to happen? We can't see God, and most of us do not hear His voice out loud, so a lot of people doubt that He really loves them.

Sometimes what gets in the way of believing God loves us is guilt. We look at things we've done and think He couldn't possibly love us when we have made big mistakes.

> A Brazilian pastor told the story of a young widow whose beautiful teenage daughter dreamed day and night about living in the big city of Rio de Janeiro instead of their small town. Her mother tried to warn her that the city could be a dangerous place. Jobs were scarce and life could be cruel. But her daughter was independent and determined. Her mother knew if she went to the big city and couldn't find work what she might do or might have to do to make a living. That's why she was heart-broken to awaken one morning to find only a note telling her that her daughter was gone.
>
> She hurriedly packed a bag and headed for the bus station to follow her to Rio. On the way to the bus, she stopped at a drugstore and sat in one of those booths where you can put quarters in and take photographs of yourself. She arrived in

> Rio with her purse full of those little photos. She went every place she thought she might find her, but without any success. Fearing the worst, she began to check all the bars, hotels or nightclubs with a reputation for street walkers or prostitutes. And everywhere she went, she left one of her photos taped on a bathroom mirror, tacked on a hotel bulletin board, stuck in the corner of a phone booth. On the back of each photo, she wrote a note to her daughter. It wasn't long before both her pictures and her money ran out and she had to go home feeling that she had failed.
>
> A few weeks later, in one of those dumpy hotels, her daughter started down the stairs. Her eyes no longer sparkled; her young face was tired. Her dream had become a nightmare. Yet she knew there was no way she could ever go home again. At the bottom of the stairs, her eye caught one of those familiar photographs taped to the lobby mirror. Removing it, she found the note on the back, "Whatever you have done, whatever you've become, it doesn't matter. Please come home." She did.[3]

This story is a lot like the parable of the prodigal son from Luke 15. In the story, a man had two sons, and the younger one asked his father for his share of his inheritance before his father died. The father gave it, and the son squandered it and ran out of money. Then a famine struck the land and he ended up getting a job feeding pigs, just wishing he could eat the pig food. Something shifted in his thinking in Luke 15:17–24:

> Coming to his senses he thought, "How many of my father's hired workers have more than enough food to eat, but here am I, dying from hunger. I shall get up and go to my father and I shall say to him, 'Father, I have sinned against heaven and against you. I no longer deserve to be called your son; treat me as you would treat one of your hired workers.'" So he got up and went back to his father.
>
> While he was still a long way off, his father caught sight of him, and was filled with compassion. He ran to his son, embraced him and kissed him. His son said to him, "Father, I have sinned against heaven and against you; I no longer deserve to be called your son." But his father ordered his servants, "Quickly bring the finest robe and put it on him; put a ring on his finger and sandals on his feet. Take the fattened calf and slaughter it. Then let us celebrate with a feast, because this son of mine was dead, and has come to life again; he was lost, and has been found." Then the celebration began.

Why did the son decide to return to his father for forgiveness? *[Let your daughter answer.]*

---

[3] Max Lucado, *No Wonder They Call Him the Savior* (Nashville, TN: Thomas Nelson, 2004), 129–131.

How did the father respond? *[Let your daughter answer.]*

When did the father start running to the son? *[Let your daughter answer.]*

The father started running to his son the minute he saw him. This was *before* the son had asked forgiveness. This is how God relates to us. He is full of mercy. He loves us completely. He runs to us and showers us with love.

But we need to take the step that the prodigal son took. He turned around and went back to his father. Which brings us back to our first point: Our heavenly Father is a gentleman, and He waits for us to turn to Him and invite Him to come close.

God's love for us doesn't depend on us being perfect. He doesn't hold us at a distance and wait for us to go and clean ourselves up. God's love isn't conditional. That is a lie.

The truth is seen in the story of the prodigal son. It's also seen in Romans 8:38–39: "For I am convinced that neither death nor life, neither angels nor demons, neither the present nor the future, nor any powers, neither height nor depth, nor anything else in all creation, will be able to separate us from the love of God that is in Christ Jesus our Lord."

What can separate us from the love of God? Nothing. There is nothing we can do that will take away God's love for us. In the words of Saint Augustine, "God loves each one of us as if there were only one of us." So let's invite Him to come close, to fill up our hearts with His love.

Discussion Questions:

Do you ever feel emptiness in your heart?

Have you asked God to fill it?

Quiet your heart. . . .

Ask your daughter for something specific that is on her heart—a dream, a worry, a troubled relationship—and pray for that desire or need.

Dear God,
Please help us to see who You really are—to know, deep in our hearts, that You are a good, good Father. Help us to trust Your plan for our lives. You have never left our side and never stop loving us. Help us to start each day remembering that we are Your daughters, and You smile on us and call us beloved. May we stop believing lies about You—especially the lie that we need to be perfect in order to be loved by You. The truth is, nothing can separate us from Your love. Help us to stop looking at our circumstances to determine whether You love us, and instead to look at the cross, and to be reminded of the lengths You went to in order to show us what we mean to You. Amen.

JOURNALING CONVERSATIONS

I feel loved when you . . .

I feel listened to when you . . .

MOTHER

DAUGHTER

NOTES

Day 9

SAVED BY THE SON

I think many times people don't give girls your age enough credit. Far too often, you are talked to as if you are unable to understand deeper things, and far too often, the focus turns to merely keeping you entertained instead of challenging you to do the things that will help you become world changers.

We keep talking about truth versus lies. It is a lie that you can't make important decisions at your age. The truth is, you can, and there is no better time than today.

I believe there is so much hope wrapped up in your heart—tremendous potential for you to make a real difference in your generation. But so much hinges on the most important decision you will ever make. That's what we're going to talk about today.

We have talked about the fact that God is a gentleman and He waits to be invited into your heart. What God wants more than anything is to have a personal relationship with you. He created every person on earth, but not every person has turned to Him and asked to have a personal relationship with Him. The truth is, most people don't have any idea how to do that.

The Catholic Church teaches us about the importance of "conversion of the heart." Conversion of heart is a *choice* that we make. Let me explain. . . .

The word *conversion* means "the act of turning." This means that conversion involves a turning away from one thing and a turning toward another. When you haven't experienced conversion of the heart, you are turned toward what *you* want. You are the one in charge, and you do what you feel is right and best at any given time. You may choose to do things that are very good for other people, but the distinction is that *you* are choosing. *You* are deciding. *You* are the one in control.

Imagine driving in a car, sitting in the driver's seat with your hands on the steering wheel. You've welcomed Jesus into the passenger's seat and have listened to His comments. But whether or not you follow His directions is really up to you. You may or may not follow them, depending on what seems right to you.

Here is what happens when you experience conversion of the heart:

You decide to *turn*, to get out of the driver's seat, move into the passenger's seat, and invite God to be the driver. Instead of seeing Him as an advice giver or someone nice to have around for the holidays, you give Him control of every aspect of your life.

More than likely, you don't find this easy to do. This is because we all struggle with letting go. We want to be the ones in charge. Conversion of the heart isn't possible without humility. Having humility means recognizing that we don't have all the solutions. It's admitting that we need help.

The truth is, sin separates us from God. No one is perfect enough to earn his or her way into God's favor and forgiveness. I would guess that Saint Teresa of Calcutta has a shorter list of sins than you or I do, but she still could not earn her way into God's favor. Her sin separated her from God, too.

"*But wait!*" I can imagine you saying. "I thought you said God loves me. I thought you said there's nothing I could do to take away His love!"

Yes, that is what I said and what we read in the Bible, and *it is true*. But we have to come to a point where we accept His love, recognizing that it isn't something we have *earned* because we are perfect. It's something that God has chosen to *give* us, even though we don't deserve it.

How did God give us His love? We see this described in 2 Corinthians 5:21: "God made him who had no sin to be sin for us, so that in him we might become the righteousness of God."

How did God make Him who had no sin to be sin for you?

Jesus accomplished this on the cross. Every sin committed, past, present, and future, was placed on Him. All of your sins. All of my sins. Jesus paid the wages of sin—the punishment of sin. He did that in our place.

This is called the divine exchange. We give Him all our sin. He died in our place, so that we don't have to. In exchange for our sin, He gives us *His virtues*; *His goodness*. But in order for that exchange to take place, you need to recognize that you need Him, that you fail, you need forgiveness, and you need a savior.

When you come before God in prayer and acknowledge these truths, He looks at your heart. He sees your desire to trust Him, to please Him, and to obey Him. He says to you, "My precious daughter, you don't have to pay for your sins. My Son, Jesus, has already done that for you. He suffered so that you wouldn't have to. I want to experience a personal relationship with you." He says, "I forgive you. I came to set you free and to give you a completely new start. The old you has gone. The new you is here! If you will stay close to me, I will give you everything you need to obey me and live the incredible life that I created you for."

God wants you to know that He has been waiting to pour His gifts into your soul. You are His beloved daughter, and He wants you to remain confident in Him. He is your loving Father. Trust Him. He will take care of everything.

Accepting this as truth is what leads you to a conversion of the heart. In Revelation 3:20, Jesus says, "Behold, I stand at the door and knock. If anyone hears my voice and opens the door, I will come in to him." You don't have to be sitting in church to open that door. You can do it today. And I pray you will.

Have you ever read the children's book *Harold and the Purple Crayon*? In this book, Harold has a magical possession, a purple crayon. Anything that he draws comes to life. So if Harold wanted a car, he'd just draw it and it would be real. If he wanted a lollipop, he'd only need to draw it and it would be in his hand.

What sorts of things would you draw if you had a magical crayon like that one? How would you draw your ideal life, your dreams, and what you most desire?

Deep down, isn't this what we want in life? We want to hold the purple crayon, and create the best circumstances possible. So we work, and we plan, and we do all that we can to achieve a life as close to our ideal as we possibly can. We like to be the ones in charge. Most people hold pretty tightly to their purple crayons.

But when we experience conversion of heart, we decide to hand our purple crayons over to God. When we do this, we are saying, "God, I want *you* to draw the picture of my life."

Is it sometimes hard to trust God with our purple crayons? Yes, sometimes it is. But I promise you, God is the best artist—the creator of the universe—and He draws the most beautiful pictures. And as the author of life, He writes a better story than we ever could.

Discussion Questions:

What sorts of things would you draw if you had a magical crayon like Harold's? How would you draw your ideal life, your dreams, and what you most desire?

Are you willing to give God your purple crayon?

Does the thought of handing God your purple crayon make you feel nervous? Why or why not?

Quiet your heart. . . .

Ask your daughter for something specific that is on her heart—a dream, a worry, a troubled relationship—and pray for that desire or need.

Dear God,
Thank You so much for loving [your daughter's name]. Thank You for giving her dreams and things that she is hoping for. Thank You for not creating her like a robot and just commanding her to love You. Thank You for giving her a choice. May she recognize that she isn't perfect, that she has sinned, and that she needs a Savior. It's hard to trust You sometimes, but help her to know that trust is a choice, and sometimes her feelings have to catch up later.
Amen.

If your daughter would like words to help her hand her purple crayon to God, she might like to pray the following:

Dear God,
I trust You. And I'm asking You to forgive me, and to fill my heart. God, I choose You. I choose to hand You my purple crayon, and to let You draw the picture of my life. Thank You for being true to Your promises. I know You are standing at the door to my heart and knocking. I'm opening up the door and asking You to come in. I'm so glad that You're the best artist—that as the creator of the universe, You will draw the most beautiful picture with my life.
Amen.

JOURNALING CONVERSATIONS

For mom: The best listening ear/person to go to for advice when I was your age was…

For daughter: If you had a problem, to whom would you go for a listening ear and advice, besides me?

MOTHER

DAUGHTER

NOTES

Day 10

EMPOWERED BY THE HOLY SPIRIT

Following Jesus means that we live the way He wants us to live. Remember when we talked about giving Jesus our purple crayon? Do you remember what that means? It means we allow Him to be the one in charge.

As we become more spiritually mature, we start to grow in our trust of Him. We can ask Him to help us to believe how much He loves us, and to believe that because of this love, He would never ask anything of us that is not for our benefit.

But living the way Jesus wants us to live isn't always easy. It isn't easy to fight against a culture that measures beauty by outward appearance. It isn't easy to reach out to the awkward or unpleasant people in our lives. It isn't easy to forgive and pray for our enemies. It isn't easy to get up and help others when we'd rather do something else. We can have all sorts of good intentions, but it can be really, really hard to consistently live the way Jesus asks us to.

To illustrate what I'm talking about, imagine that there's a glove sitting in front of you. It's a work glove, which means it was created for work. That's what it was designed for. But without a hand in it, it's not very impressive. Words of encouragement wouldn't help the glove to be more productive. Even though it's designed for work, a glove can't do that work until a living hand is placed inside it and fills it up.

That's how the Christian life works. We are unable to live the way God asks in our own strength. We have the capacity for it, we were made for it, but we don't have the strength to do it. We need something to fill us up, something that fills us with power that we wouldn't have otherwise.

The times when we fall on our faces, the times when we fail to love the way we should, remind us that we need something more than our good intentions. This was a lesson that Saint Peter learned the hard way.

The night of Jesus' arrest and trial, during the Last Supper, Jesus told His disciples that all of them were going to have their faith shaken. This really bothered Peter, who said, "Even though all of the others might have their faith shaken, mine never will be."

Jesus looked right at him and said, "Before the cock crows twice, this very night, you will deny me three times."

But Peter, full of confidence in himself, said, "No way. Even if I was asked to die with you, I would never deny you."

Do you remember the story of what happened that night? How brave was he? What did Saint Peter do? The Bible tells us that he denied even knowing Jesus. Why? Because he was afraid.

We read in Luke 22:61 that the third time Peter denied Jesus, Jesus turned and looked at him. I wonder what that felt like for Peter. Can you imagine the sick feeling you get in your stomach when you've gossiped about someone and then the person finds out what you have said? I'm sure Peter felt a million times worse than that. Luke 22:62 said that he ran out and began to weep bitterly. I haven't heard a grown man cry very many times, but I am sure that Peter's sorrow was painful to even listen to.

But in that moment, Peter had been given a real gift. He had learned the lesson that on his own, he wasn't nearly as strong as he'd thought. If he was going to follow Jesus, he would need something more than good intentions. He was going to need something more than good friends.

He got that something more on Pentecost, and everything changed. In the book of Acts, we read of the Holy Spirit falling on the disciples like tongues of fire. When Peter was filled with the Holy Spirit, he was suddenly able to do things he'd never been able to do before. He stepped out before a massive crowd—one that might have wanted to kill him or arrest him—and he spoke incredibly bravely and boldly about Jesus.

On our own, we can't do very much. All our best intentions usually stay just that—good intentions, good ideas.

When we fail to do what we hoped or wished we could do, we often start to believe the lie: I just can't help my bad habits; I can't change; I'm never going to be any different; it's just too hard.

But the truth is found in Philippians 4:13: "I can do all things through Christ who strengthens me."

On your own, you can't obey everything Jesus asks of you. It's too difficult. That's why He sent the Holy Spirit to you when you were baptized. And then He fills you with the Holy Spirit when you are confirmed. He knows you can't do it alone.

So He sent the Holy Spirit to literally live inside you. He is your comforter, your counselor, your helper, your intercessor, your strengthener. When we whisper, "I can't," He says, "I know. I know you can't. But I can. And I have been sent to you to help you. And with my help, when you call on me in prayer, you can do all the things I ask of you."

The Holy Spirit is willing to do so much for you, but He is a gentleman. He waits to be invited in. You can decide to just keep Him at the entryway of your house, or you can invite Him to come all the way in. That's what I pray you will do.

Discussion Questions:

Have you ever tried to love the way God wants you to and found that you just weren't able?

Have you ever asked the Holy Spirit to help you do what God has asked? If you have, did prayer make a difference?

Are you willing to ask the Holy Spirit to fill you up from the top of your head to the tips of your toes?

Quiet your heart. . . .

Ask your daughter for something specific that is on her heart—a dream, a worry, a troubled relationship—and pray for that desire or need.

Dear God,
Help us to stop repeating the lie, "I can't change." Because of the Holy Spirit living in us, we can do whatever You ask of us. As Saint Ephraem said, "Prayer draws into the soul the Holy Spirit." Please help us grow in humility so that we remember to ask for the Holy Spirit's help. Whether or not we are asking for this help can be seen by how often we turn to You in prayer. Help us to remember to pray more often. Thank You for caring about all the details of our lives. We don't need to wait and only ask You about the big things. You care about all of it, and You just wait to be invited into the

details of our lives. You are always willing to help, and You always make a difference. Thank You for caring about us in this way.
Amen.

JOURNALING CONVERSATIONS

Has fear ever prevented you from pursuing a dream? What was the fear? What was the dream?

MOTHER

DAUGHTER

NOTES

Day 11

PRAYER

So many of us think of prayer as something we *do*. We repeat words that we've memorized, or we try to come up with something that sounds spiritual. But when we approach prayer this way, we're missing what it's meant to be.

Each day, we've been talking about lies and truth. Our lie today is a tricky one, because there's some truth mixed into it: All I need to do is say the Our Father and I'm good.

What part of this lie do you think is true and good? There's nothing bad or wrong with the Our Father. It's a good prayer, and it's actually how Jesus taught us to pray. So why would I say it's a lie to believe all you need to do is say the Our Father and you're good?

We find the truth of what I'm getting at in the Bible, in the very place where we're taught how to pray the Our Father, in Matthew 6:5–13. In verse 8, Jesus says, "In praying, do not babble like the pagans, who think that they will be heard because of their many words. Do not be like them."

Jesus urged His listeners not to turn prayer into a theatrical production. He pointed out how some people prayed in certain ways just to get attention from those around them. But this isn't anything that's going to impress God. God wants us to go to a quiet space. He doesn't want us to "role-play" in front of Him. He doesn't want an actress's performance; He wants time with His daughter. Jesus said that God wants you to be there as simply and as honestly as you can be. He wants your focus to be on Him, not on how good you look or how impressive you sound. He doesn't need a perfectly formed prayer or eloquence. He knows what you need, which means that you can pray very simply. Jesus taught all those things before teaching His followers the words of the Our Father.

The *way* we should pray is going to have everything to do with *why* we are praying. What are some reasons why people pray?
[Possible answers: because we are supposed to, because we're around people who are praying, because we need help]

Do you know what gives God so much pleasure? He loves it when we pray because we want to connect with Him because He is our best friend.

Think about one of your close friends. How strong would your relationship be if you never talked to her? Or if you never told her how you were feeling? How do you think your friendship would do if you got mad and gave up on the friendship every time your friend didn't fix things perfectly when you had a problem?

There is no one who loves you more perfectly than Jesus. No one. And He wants your friendship. Just like with your girlfriends, if you never talk to Jesus and share with Him how you really are, you won't be very close to Him.

I want to talk to you about a tool that can help you to stay close to Jesus—not just at Mass, but every day at home. It's a prayer journal. *[We have a BLAZE prayer journal available for purchase, but you can use any journal.]* I encourage you to use a prayer journal each morning—to start your day by talking to God about how you are feeling. He is interested in the state of your heart and always cares about how you are. Just start off by finishing this sentence: "God, today I'm feeling . . ."

Then you can take time to write out a thank-you to Him for who He is and what He's done. After this, you can ask Him for what you need, but since we've learned that God knows what we need even better than we do, we know we won't always get what we ask for.

After using your journal for a while, you'll find that what you have is a book of letters to God. When you look back at old entries, you'll be able to see how faithful He has been to you—that He has never left you and has always come through for you. Writing it all down helps you to remember and notice answers to prayer. This will help grow your trust in God.

Saint Ignatius said, "We must speak to God as a friend speaks to a friend." That's what I think a prayer journal helps us start to do.

In your prayer journal, I recommend using the word ACTS to help you to pray:

Adoration: thanking God for who He is

Confession: asking God for forgiveness for specific things

Thanksgiving: thanking God for what He's done or what He's given

Supplication: asking God for what we need

Just as Jesus encouraged His listeners to go somewhere quiet to pray, I want to challenge you to do the same. What might change if you made a commitment to get up just ten minutes earlier each day to spend time talking to God? Don't you think your friendship with Him would grow closer?

Discussion Questions:

Have you found it hard or boring to pray?

Which type of prayer would be a new experience for you—sharing your feelings, thanking God, praising Him, confessing sin, or asking for what you need?

Are you willing to get up ten minutes earlier to start your day with prayer?

Quiet your heart. . . .

Ask your daughter for something specific that is on her heart—a dream, a worry, a troubled relationship—and pray for that desire or need.

Dear God,
Help us to look at prayer the way You want us to. Instead of seeing it as a duty, something that we mindlessly recite, or a box to be checked off, may we see it as the best way to build our friendship with You. Give us the self-discipline to set aside time in our day to come to You, quietly, to pray. Help us to bring our whole selves—our feelings, our gratitude, our fears, and our needs. You care about every detail of our lives. You are always ready to listen. You are always available. Even though You created the world, even though You hold everything together, You still take time for us. May we never take that for granted.
Amen.

JOURNALING CONVERSATIONS

What are three of your favorite books? Which character would you like to be if you could jump into the pages?

MOTHER

DAUGHTER

Day 12

THE HOLE IN YOUR HEART

PREP:

Before your time with your daughter, take two pieces of construction paper in different colors and draw a heart on each. On one of the hearts, write the words emotions, dreams, goals, hopes, passions, *and* devotion. *On the other heart, write the word* boyfriend. *Glue the two pieces of paper together with the hearts/words facing out so you can still see them. It's important that the glue be fully dry before you continue. Begin your time together by discussing the following question:*

Do you see more examples of boy/girl drama in your class or good examples of boy/girl dating relationships?

[Hand your daughter the two hearts.]

You have two hearts in your hand. One represents your heart, which is full of emotions, dreams, goals, hopes, passions, and devotion. The other heart represents a boyfriend. These two hearts are glued together, giving us a visual for what can happen when two people are dating. Now try to separate the two hearts, without getting any of the paper from one heart on the other one.

[Note: If the glue has dried, this will be an impossible task. Inevitably, bits of one paper end up on the other.]

Our hearts can stick to each other when we are in a relationship. There's something called "heart glue," in which you can become connected to a boy emotionally or physically, and when you separate, you leave a little piece of yourself with that person, and it can really hurt.

Everyone wants to feel loved, and there is nothing wrong with that. We were made to crave love. The problem is where we look for that love. If we aren't getting the love we need from our families or friends, it's easy to look to boys to fill us up. God knows that this can lead us into tricky territory. In Proverbs 4:23 He tells us, "Above all else, guard your heart, for it is the wellspring of life."

Another word for wellspring is *source*. This means that your heart is the source of your life. If your heart stops beating, you stop living. That's the physical side of it. Spiritually, we say that our heart is where the Holy Spirit lives. Emotionally, it's where our feelings dwell. This verse is telling us to protect our hearts, because they are so important.

Our hearts were created with a hole that is meant to be filled with God. Only He can satisfy what feels empty inside us. When we look for another person to fill it, we are always disappointed, and sometimes *[indicate the construction paper hearts]* we get hurt in the process. Saint Augustine said, "You have made us for yourself, and our hearts are restless till they find their rest in you." We can get into all sorts of bad situations and our hearts can get broken if we don't realize this.

Our lie for today is:
I need a boyfriend to be happy.

The truth is found in Colossians 2:10:
"You are complete in Christ."

Without a personal relationship with Jesus, our hearts are like a puzzle with one piece missing. We sometimes think a boy will be the missing piece. But he never will be. The missing piece is always God. But He'll never completely satisfy us if we keep looking for someone else to fill us up. He's a gentleman. He won't force His way into our hearts.

But one thing I can promise you, only God will be perfectly tender with your heart. People, even the best ones, will make a mistake at some point and disappoint you. Only God will love you *without* fail, with a steadfast, faithful, and merciful love.

What do you think are some ways that you can guard your heart?

[Some ideas: wait to date, invest more time in your girlfriends than in a boyfriend, be careful what you share, make good choices physically so things don't get even more intense]

Do you know that the Bible is your very own love note from God? It's loaded with verses that are from His heart to yours. So when you are wondering if maybe a boy is what is missing in your life, I want you to look at these Bible verses. Do you feel ugly? Read Song of Songs 4:7 to find out how God sees your beauty. Do you feel unlovable? Read Jeremiah 31:3. Are you afraid? Psalm 139:13–16 is God's message to you. When you feel alone, I encourage you to read Isaiah 41:10. Do you need a hero? No one rescues like Jesus, and you can read about that in John 14:1–3.

The missing piece isn't a boyfriend. The only one who will complete you is Jesus.

Discussion Questions:

What do you think is a good age to start dating?

What is something that is positive about dating?

What is something that is harmful?

Quiet your heart. . . .

Ask your daughter for something specific that is on her heart—a dream, a worry, a troubled relationship—and pray for that desire or need.

Dear God,
Help [your daughter's name] to truly believe that she is "complete in Christ" [Colossians 2:10]. Help her to go to You first when she feels empty, alone, or afraid. Instead of wanting boys to affirm that she is worth fighting for and that she is beautiful enough to be chosen, help her to remember that You have already fought for her and that You have chosen her. Remind her, Holy Spirit, that You are the missing puzzle piece, and that no one will be more tender with her heart than You. You love her, not because You want something from her, but because You want to fill her and bless her.
Amen.

JOURNALING CONVERSATIONS

What do you think is the purpose of dating?

MOTHER

DAUGHTER

Day 13

FRIENDSHIP KILLERS

We all long for a friend who will be loyal to us no matter what. But too often, what we experience instead is competition, comparison, gossip, and fakeness instead of authenticity and faithfulness.

If I were to ask a group of girls if they had ever been hurt, betrayed, or disappointed by a friend, a lot of hands would go up. I know there would be a great deal of hurt in that room. I wish this wasn't the case, but all too often, girls start to wonder if friendships with girls are safe. This can cause them to gravitate toward boys, who seem a little less complicated. There's nothing wrong with being friends with boys, but when that is what we choose because we don't trust the girls we know, we have a problem.

My prayer is that you and the girls in your life will start learning to treat each other better. There is nothing like a good friend who has known us for years and years. I hope you have friendships that last a long time—friendships that are healthy and bring out the best in you. But the hurt that is all too common among girls can really get in the way of that happening, so I want to talk about some friendship killers.

Here is today's lie:
It doesn't matter what I say or think about a friend as long as she doesn't find out about it.

Here is today's truth:
Friendship killers are stealthy; they do damage even when things happen behind the scenes.

What do I mean by friendship killers? Let's look at three of the most common.

Friendship Killer 1: Comparison

Nothing kills a good friendship like comparison because it gets in the way of our being happy for one another. And what type of comparisons do we tend to make? Do I compare my best self with your best self? No. When I compare, I compare me at my worst with you at your best. I look at what I don't like about myself and compare it to someone else's pretty hair, athletic ability, good grades, or nice family.

When I compare in this way, am I basing my comparison on a realistic picture of both our lives? Am I seeing everything about the other's life? No, but we forget this in the heat of the moment, and the harm is done.

When we compare and then feel we don't measure up, we often fall into the second friendship killer:

Friendship Killer 2: Gossip

Why do people gossip? Maybe it's because we aren't feeling so great about ourselves, and sharing something juicy about someone makes us feel a little more interesting. Or perhaps we're feeling insecure, full of awareness of all that's wrong with us, so we decide to pull another person down, too. Misery loves company.

It's interesting to note that the Hebrew word for *gossip* in the Old Testament means "traveling with a confidence." Have you ever experienced that firsthand? How did it feel? *[Let your daughter answer.]*

We read in Proverbs 16:28, "A troublemaker plants seeds of strife; gossip separates the best of friends." If someone has gossiped about you, you know the truth of that verse. Gossip can cause significant damage to a friendship.

Proverbs 18:8 tells us, "The words of a talebearer (gossip) are like dainty morsels; they sink into one's inmost being." Isn't that so true? How often do we forget gossip that we've heard? Not very often. We remember. It was interesting. Whether we wanted it to or not, those words traveled deep within us and lodged in our inmost parts. Just as it's hard to stop eating Cool Ranch Doritos after we have one, it's hard to shut the door on gossip once we've taken the first bite. So what's the solution? Don't even take a bite. Walk away. Be brave when someone starts gossiping and say, "I don't want to talk about her if she's not here to give her side of the story."

Friendship Killer 3: Being Fake

Another friendship killer is being fake. It can be scary to reveal who we truly are. What if this friend doesn't end up being trustworthy? Or what if she doesn't like what she sees when she sees the real me? We all fear rejection. So all too often, we wear masks. We think to ourselves, "So what if it isn't the real me? I don't want to be rejected!" But is a friendship between two girls who are wearing masks particularly satisfying? No. Is it real? Not really.

What is the real problem underlying all of these friendship killers? **We measure our worth by the wrong things.** If we base our worth on the quality and level of our accomplishments, or if our worth is based on what we look like or what people think of us, then we are hindered in our ability to love. Instead of lovingly focusing on the other person, we wind up scoping out the competition.

I want you to think about two questions:

What defines you?
Who are you?

When you define yourself as God's beloved daughter, everything changes. It means that you enter any relationship coming from a place of already being deeply loved—of knowing you are precious to God, full of grace. When you ask God to fill what is empty inside, you don't place unrealistic expectations on your friends. It also can give us the confidence to be real. When we come to recognize that we are made in the image of God, then we begin to embrace the truth that we are likable. We have something to offer. We have something to give.

In a true friendship you can say, "This is who I am."

A true friendship is a relationship in which you have the freedom to share who you are and to be truly vulnerable. You can let a friend see all of you, down to the core.

I'd like to challenge you to choose one of the friendship killers—comparison, gossip, or being fake—and commit to eradicating it from your life. But don't try to do this in your own strength. Ask the Holy Spirit to help you. Make this one of the focuses of your prayer time. Journal about your feelings and what is making comparison, gossip, and fakeness so tempting. Ask God to help you in this area of your life, and prepare to experience far more freedom and happiness in your friendships.

Discussion Questions:

Which of the friendship killers would you like to eradicate from your life?

Which of your friendships has the least amount of drama?

What would you say if someone asked you, "Who are you? How do you define yourself?"

Quiet your heart. . . .

Ask your daughter for something specific that is on her heart—a dream, a worry, a troubled relationship—and pray for that desire or need.

Dear God,
We all are tempted to compare. And without fail, comparison steals our joy. Help us to recognize that this robs us of friendships that could be a wonderful gift in our lives. Help us to notice where we are comparing (on social media? at school? on the sports field?) and to ask for Your help to see ourselves through Your eyes. Give us the courage to say no to gossip. Help us to refuse to talk about someone if he or she is not there to defend him- or herself. Help us to be brave and real instead of faking fine. But give us wisdom to know which friends can be trusted with our hearts.
Amen.

JOURNALING CONVERSATIONS

What do you think are the most important qualities to look for in a friend?

MOTHER

DAUGHTER

NOTES

Day 14

HOW TO BE A FRIEND

We're going to continue talking about friendship—specifically, how you can be a better friend to others. One thing I know for sure: It can be really hard to put another person's needs above our own. So often we go into friendship with mixed motives. We want to be filled up. We want to be noticed. We want to be loved. We want to be encouraged.

Our lie for today:
It's all about me.

The truth is found in Philippians 2:3–4: "Do nothing out of selfishness or out of vainglory; rather, humbly regard others as more important than yourselves, each looking out not for his own interests, but also everyone for those of others." In these verses, Saint Paul is saying that instead of starting with what we want for ourselves, we should look at how we can help others.

How do we do that? Let's look at three things we can do to be a good friend to others.

1. We show up.

   What do I mean by that? Am I just talking about your body being in a certain place at a certain time? No, I'm talking about you showing up totally—with your whole, real self. I'm talking about being *present.*

   Have you ever been with a group of friends and noticed that everyone was on their phone? You were all together, but not really connecting. And that's a lost opportunity, because friendships are built when people talk, look each other in the eye, and show the other person that he or she matters more than whatever entertainment is on the screen.

   When you are with a friend, I want to encourage you to show her how much you care about her by putting her first and showing her that she matters to you—by putting your cell phone down. Really talk to her. Use her name. Ask her questions. Listen to her answers. Use your phone to plan, but use your face to connect.

2. Forgive willingly and often.

In any friendship, there are going to be things said that occasionally rub the wrong way. When this happens, we are wise to ask ourselves, "Can I overlook this?" Proverbs 19:11 says that a wise person is patient and able to overlook an offense. We don't have to make a big deal of every little hurt. Some things we can just quietly forgive.

Bigger things need some discussion. But by this, I mean discussion with the person who hurt you—not everyone else on the periphery of the situation. Something that can help us to forgive is to remember that hurting people hurt people. When we try to imagine what it's like to walk in another person's shoes, when we think about the fact that everyone has insecurities, fears, and hurts, we grow in our ability to forgive.

But I don't mean that you should just stuff what you're feeling. The more you are able to tell someone they hurt you, the better off you'll be.

Sometimes we think someone has to tell us they are sorry in order for us to forgive them. That's not the case. We can forgive whether or not someone asks for forgiveness. When we refuse to forgive, it's like drinking poison and expecting the other person to get sick. Refusing to forgive hardens our hearts. In the end, it hurts us more than others.

Sometimes *we're* the ones who need to be forgiven. When that's the case, it's good to remember that there's a big difference between a halfhearted "Sorry" and someone sincerely asking, "Will you forgive me?" I encourage you to be quick to ask for forgiveness instead of hoping that the bad feelings and awkwardness will just go away.

Lastly, in friendship, we . . .

3. Earn the right to be heard.

Sometimes, in order to be a truly loving friend, we need to speak some truth that might be hard to hear. Some people call this speaking the truth in love. This is different from being negative or critical. If we aren't sure if speaking up about something would be kind or if it would be critical and negative, we can look at our motivation.

Why do we feel a need to say something? Where are we coming from? Are we angry? If so, we should let our anger settle before we speak. Are we confronting our friend because we truly care for her and want what's best for her, or do we just want to get something off our chests? Sometimes this is hard to figure out, so be sure to spend time in prayer beforehand. You can say to God, "Help me to know whether I should say something, and if I should, then help me to say it in a loving way." This allows God to prepare your heart by helping you to check your own motivation, and it gives you the opportunity to ask the Holy Spirit to prepare your friend's heart, as well.

It's also good to remember that we earn the right to be heard. If our relationship has been characterized by criticism, or if we haven't been building up our friend, it's likely that the truth spoken in love will be hard to hear. The majority of our interactions should be building each other up, encouraging, and loving. Does your friend know that you would do anything for her, and that you want what's best for her? If not, she is likely to react defensively to the conversation.

In addition, any conversation like this is best done face-to-face. Letters and texts can all be easily misunderstood.

It's been said that a true friend accepts who you are, but also helps you become who you should be. Being that kind of a friend won't always be easy, but in the end, it's worth it. Saint Teresa of Calcutta said, "A life not lived for others is not a life." But when we wake up each day determined to be a good friend and put others' needs before our own, our hearts feel full and satisfied.

Discussion Questions:

Which of these things do you find hardest to do—being present, forgiving others, or earning the right to be heard?

Have you ever had to speak the truth in love to a friend?

How do you think you would react if someone spoke the truth in love to you?

Quiet your heart. . . .

Ask your daughter for something specific that is on her heart—a dream, a worry, a troubled relationship—and pray for that desire or need.

Dear God,
Instead of focusing on what we want from our friends—how we want them to make us feel—help us to think about how we can be kinder, more honest, and more helpful. May we put You first, then others, and then ourselves. May we be quick to forgive, and slow to become angry. May we truly show up in friendship, putting our phones away and looking people in the eye. May You be our example in friendship, Jesus. May we learn to love like You.
Amen

JOURNALING CONVERSATIONS

Why do you think people say or do mean things?

MOTHER

DAUGHTER

NOTES

Day 15

CHOOSING FRIENDS

"There is nothing on this earth more to be prized than true friendship." —Saint Thomas Aquinas

The Bible has so much to say about friendship. Friendship is important—not just because it gives us comfort and joy, but because of the way it impacts who we become. We read in Proverbs 13:10, "Walk with wise and you become wise, but the companion of fools fares badly." We become like the people we are surrounded by.

Ideally, we would all experience the true friendship Saint Thomas Aquinas wrote about. As it says in Proverbs 17:17, "A friend is a friend at all times, and a brother is born for the time of adversity." We want the kind of friend who is loyal to us in both the good times and the bad. In Luke 6:31, Jesus shares a great principle of friendship with the words, "Do to others as you would have them do to you." Who wouldn't want this? We know what true friendship feels like, but we aren't always so certain how to make sure that is what we experience.

It really hurts when someone sets out to hurt us, but nothing is more painful than a friend turning on a friend. Whoever we allow to be the closest to us has the greatest potential to hurt us. Our good friends know a lot about us, and we have trusted them. So if they do something to betray us, the pain goes really deep. No one is perfect; there are always times in friendship when hurts happen. But if that is the norm in a friendship, then it's probably time to take a look at the people you are choosing as your closest friends.

Even Jesus took time to do this. He had many followers, but He spent all night in prayer before He narrowed down that group to twelve disciples. He asked God whom He should surround Himself with. He then chose three of the twelve (Peter, James, and John) to be the closest of all.

Pay attention to who is in your inner circle of friends. Jesus did. When the chips are down and you are in a crisis, you need a friend who can speak the truth in love and guide you to the right path. Too often, our friends just say what makes us feel good.

I want to share with you some qualities of a good friend. These are things you want to see in the people you surround yourself with. But more important, these are the qualities you want to see in yourself. Think of it on both these levels when I share these character traits.

Today's lie:
The best qualities to look for in a friend are popularity and fun.

Today's truth:
The best friends are kind, encouraging, honest, and grace-giving.

Kind
Her words build you up; they don't tear you down. She cares about you and doesn't compete with you. She doesn't change her best friend each week, because she recognizes that it messes with girls' hearts. You can rely on her. She is steady and loyal.

Encouraging
She's there for you in the good times and the bad. She stands up for you if someone is talking behind your back.

Honest and up front
A good friend does not mess with your mind. She is straightforward. What you see is what you get. She doesn't play games with you. She isn't hot and cold—she's steady. Because of this, you feel good after you've been with her. You don't go home and then spend hours trying to figure out what she meant or what she was thinking. A friend who is super complicated and exhausting is not honest and upfront.

Grace-giving
This last quality is a really tough one, and it comes when we mature; it's a sign of growing up. When we are still immature, it's almost impossible to do it.

A truly good friend sees the best in you. She sees who you want to be, even if you sometimes fall short of who that is. She recognizes that *everyone is doing the best they can.* This is a mark of real emotional security. You can only do this if you are able to look past how you are feeling in the moment to recognize that everyone is dealing with their own set of hurts, and we so rarely see the whole picture. This is why it's so important for us to not be quick to judge. It's also why we need to be quick to forgive. We never have all the facts. If we did, we'd be much kinder to each other. A grace giver offers mercy and kindness even when it doesn't seem to be deserved, because she recognizes that everyone is fighting some kind of a battle. Another person's life is rarely as easy as it might appear.

Discussion Questions:

What qualities do you look for in a friend?

Are your closest friends kind, encouraging, honest, and grace-giving? Are you?

In which of these areas would you like to improve?

Quiet your heart. . . .

Ask your daughter for something specific that is on her heart—a dream, a worry, a troubled relationship—and pray for that desire or need.

Dear God,
Help us to choose our friends wisely. May we truly believe the truth of Proverbs 13:10, that when we walk with the wise, we become wise. We reflect our friends and become like them, for better or worse. May our closest circle of friends be reflective of the qualities we talked about today: kindness, honesty, encouragement, and giving grace. Instead of judging others, may we all recognize that the majority of the time, everyone is just doing the best that he or she can. But help us to not just look for friends with these qualities; help us to *be* friends with these qualities. Help us to be more like You—to love the way that You do, Jesus. Thank You for placing the Holy Spirit in our hearts to help us to do this. May we take the time to ask Him to love through us.
Amen.

JOURNALING CONVERSATIONS

Which things about the two of you are similar? Which things are different?

MOTHER

DAUGHTER

Day 16

THE EUCHARIST

Have you ever felt alone? Have you ever felt alone in a room full of people? It isn't a nice feeling. In fact, Saint Theresa of Calcutta said, "Loneliness and the feeling of being unwanted is the most terrible poverty."

After World War II, many babies had been orphaned because of the bombing and fighting across Europe. Orphanages were formed to care for them, and the workers there made sure the babies were fed and clothed. They thought that was all the babies needed, but a number of them starting getting sick and dying. The caretakers termed it "failure to thrive" and couldn't figure out what was causing it. But everything changed when they started picking the babies up and just holding them. The physical touch and face-to-face connection made all the difference, because the babies—and we as well—were made for intimacy. We can literally die from being alone.

But being touched isn't the only thing that we need. We also long to be understood. Have you ever felt like no one understands you? What does that feel like? *[Let your daughter answer.]*

Our lie for today is one that a lot of people believe: I am alone and no one understands me.

But the truth is, Jesus loves you and has not left you alone. He promises this in Hebrews 13:5: "Never will I leave you; never will I forsake you."

But look around. Can you see Him? Where is He?

When we are feeling lonely, we want someone to be with us, to be near us. We want to see and touch someone. We might wonder how this works with God. He doesn't have a body that we can see and recognize the way we can see the body of a friend.

Jesus knew we would feel this way, so do you know what He said the night before He died? He gathered the apostles together, broke the bread, lifted it up, and in Luke 22:19 He said, "This is my body, which is given for you."

As Catholics, we believe this is when Jesus instituted the Eucharist. This is when He told us just how He would make sure that we were never alone.

But a lot of people believe that Jesus was just talking symbolically. They think He didn't really mean that the bread became His body. They think it's just a symbol. So why do Catholics believe it actually becomes His body?

Much of what Catholics believe about the Eucharist comes from a firm belief that Jesus truly meant what He said in John 6. This story takes place the day after His miracle of the multiplication of the loaves and fishes. A boy had five barley loaves and two fish, and Jesus multiplied them so that about five thousand men (plus women and children) were fed, with twelve baskets of bread and fish left over.

The next day, the people had come back because they were hungry again. They remembered His miracle from the day before. When they asked Jesus for something to eat, He said, "The bread of God is that which comes down from heaven and gives life to the world."

The people said they wanted that bread. Jesus replied, "I am the bread of life. Whoever comes to me will never be hungry, and whoever believes in me will never be thirsty."

When He said this, the people in the crowd started to complain. "Isn't this just Jesus?" they said. "A man just like you or me? We know his mom. We know his dad. How can he claim to have come down from heaven?"

But instead of backing down in response to their words, Jesus spoke even more boldly. He didn't take back or try to clarify His words; He amped them up. He said again, "I am the bread of life." He talked about how manna had sustained the Israelites in the Old Testament but that they all eventually died. He claimed that if they would eat the bread that was *Him*, they would live forever. "Whoever eats of this bread will live forever; and the bread that I will give for the life of the world is my flesh."

The people responded in John 6:52 by asking, "How can this man give us his flesh to eat?"

Did it seem like the people thought He was speaking symbolically? No. They were taking Him literally.

Clearly, Jesus' words weren't winning Him any popularity contests. He could have downplayed what He had previously said, or changed the subject. But that's not how He responded. In verse 53, Jesus said that unless they ate the flesh of the Son of Man and drank His blood, they wouldn't have life in them. He said His flesh was true food, and His blood was true drink, and that whoever ate His flesh and drank His blood would be with Him forever and have eternal life.

Do you know what happened as a result of Jesus' words? People walked away. People left Him. They left and no longer accompanied Him. Make no mistake, Jesus didn't watch them walk away with indifference. He came to seek and save the lost. His love for each of those souls was so huge that He was soon to die for them.

If they had simply misunderstood Him, don't you think He would have chased them down the road to clarify? But if He had meant what He said, and had simply been telling them the truth He had been waiting throughout the Old Testament to reveal, then He would have had to let them respond as they chose. He never has been one to force Himself on anyone.

Father Mike Schmitz put it pretty strongly when he said, "If you don't want the Eucharist, you don't want Jesus."

You may wonder if everyone who receives the Eucharist has the same experience. The answer is no. Theologian Peter Kreeft nails it with this explanation:

> Sacraments are like hoses. They are the channels of the living water of God's grace. Our faith is like opening the faucet. We can open it a lot, a little, or not at all. When the faucet handle is turned off, no water flows to us, even though the water is still objectively present. When it is "turned on" by faith, the water flows out and into us and we get wet.[4]

No, not everyone has the same experience at Communion, but it's up to us how open we want to be. In the words of Saint Thérèse of Lisieux, "Do you realize that Jesus is there in the tabernacle expressly for you—for you alone? He burns with the desire to come into your heart." We don't go to Mass out of obligation; we go to meet Jesus.

One of the lies we talked about earlier is that you are too young to make big decisions. The truth is, you can set an example for adults when you understand and live out these truths. This was the case with a story told of a twelve-year-old girl in China. When the communists took over China, they tried to rid the country of all religion, especially Christianity. They came into a parish and locked up the priest in the rectory. As he

---

[4] Peter Kreeft, *Jesus Shock* (Singer Island, FL: Beacon Publishing, 2008), 113.

looked out the window, he was horrified to see them burst into the church, where they smashed things up and threw the tabernacle on the ground. All the sacred hosts spilled out on the floor. The soldiers told the people to leave this place—that worship here was over and they weren't allowed back. The priest knew exactly how many hosts were in there: thirty-two. He didn't know what to do other than to watch over the Body of Christ and pray.

The twelve-year-old girl had been praying in the back of the church and saw everything that happened. That night, the priest saw her slip back into the church. She had been taught that she needed to prepare her heart for an hour before receiving the Eucharist, and that she should only receive it on her tongue. So she sat in prayer for an hour and then bent to the floor, picking up one host with her tongue, and slipped out into the night.

She did the same thing night after night. Afraid that the soldiers would see her, the priest prayed for her protection. On the last night, when she came to receive the final host, she made a noise and alerted the soldier. He was infuriated that she had continued to worship and had ignored their orders, and in his anger, he beat the girl to death with the butt of his rifle. She was martyred protecting the Eucharist.

Thankfully, we live in a country where we can worship freely. But we still have a choice. Will we look at the Eucharist as a symbol? Will we open the fire hose only a little bit because we're distracted and thinking about other things? Or will we truly worship, thanking Jesus that He loves us so much that He made sure we would never be left alone?

You are not alone. That is a lie. The truth is, you are known and understood by Jesus. He is with you, and He waits for you in the tabernacle. He longs to spend time with you. I pray you don't keep Him waiting.

Discussion Questions:

How do you typically receive the sacrament of the Eucharist?

Do you open the faucet a lot or a little?

What do you think might help you to turn the faucet on full blast?

Quiet your heart. . . .

Ask your daughter for something specific that is on her heart—a dream, a worry, a troubled relationship—and pray for that desire or need.

Dear God,
Thank You so much for never leaving us. When we are feeling lonely and like no one understands us, help us to remember that You know the very deepest parts of us and always understand. You see the things that no one else does. You actually understand us better than we understand ourselves. When we start to think that we are all alone, we can ask the Holy Spirit to speak in our hearts, reminding us of the truth that You are with us. Help us to change the way we look at going to Mass. May we not consider it an obligation, but an invitation to come and spend time with the one who totally understands us and loves us. May we open up the fire hose all the way before receiving the Eucharist by telling You that our hearts are wide open and inviting You in to fill them.
Amen.

JOURNALING CONVERSATIONS

Ten things I'd love to do with you:

MOTHER

DAUGHTER

Day 17

NO COMPROMISE

As we go through these readings, I hope that you have been growing in your understanding of how much God loves you. You don't *earn* His love; you *have* His love, because you are His precious daughter. He's a good, good Father and His love is *not* conditional on anything or anyone.

But because He is a good, good Father, He wants you to have the very best life possible. He wants you to make choices that will keep your heart whole (remember the ripped paper hearts?) and that will keep you close to Him. He doesn't want you to do things that will ultimately hurt you or leave you empty. Because of that, He tells you which choices are going to lead to the best life and which choices will lead to heartache.

In the words of author Kari Kampakis, "Your reputation is only as good as your worst choice, and left unchecked, poor choices can create damage that's hard to recover from. You and your name will be joined at the hip forever. By making a conscientious choice to protect it, you can honor your name and save yourself a lot of grief."[5]

The thing with little compromises is that they desensitize us, so the bigger compromises become easier to make. It's a snowball effect: What starts out small grows bigger and gains momentum. Reputations are built choice by choice.

Our lie for today:
Compromising what I know is right won't matter this one time.

The truth: "A good name is more desirable than great riches; to be esteemed is better than silver or gold." Proverbs 22:1

Our moment-by-moment choices are forming our reputation for today and tomorrow. A good name is hard to rebuild—not impossible, but really difficult. Remember what we said about gossip being like a choice morsel that goes deep within us (Proverbs

---

[5] Kari Kampakis, *10 Ultimate Truths Girls Should Know* (Nashville, TN: Thomas Nelson, 2014), 48.

18:8)? That's what happens when our compromises become known to others. They become a part of our reputation, and they get lodged in the hearts of other people. The choices we make stick in other people's memories. In the words of Benjamin Franklin, "It takes many good deeds to build a good reputation, and only one bad one to lose it."

One of the most important things to do if we are going to make good decisions that protect our reputation has to do with our choice of friends. In 1 Corinthians 15:33 we are reminded, "Bad company ruins good morals."

When you're getting to know people, look for warning signs and remember, bad choices usually look exciting and fun to begin with. When someone suggests doing something that is a little edgy or that skates close to the limit of what you know is wrong, there will often be something appealing about the choice. There will be a lot of laughter and maybe a little thrill of excitement, combined with the realization that if you bow out, you'll be labeled "no fun" and might be excluded in the future. But whether someone makes things exciting, fun, or humorous should not be our litmus test for who we should be hanging out with.

When you feel uneasy, pay attention. That is the Holy Spirit within you telling you to stop and think about the choice you are about to make. The funny feeling in your stomach? That is a gift from God. A warning sign. A red flag.

Does this mean that God expects us to be perfect? No. There is always grace. There is always forgiveness. But genuine confession isn't just saying I'm sorry that I did something in the past; it's promising I won't continue to do it in the future.

Will people hold some things over our heads forever? Maybe. So we always need to remember that God's opinion is the only one that ultimately counts. But His desire for us is that we make the choices that keep our hearts whole. He never stops loving us or giving us second chances, but we break His heart when we ignore the way He's asked us to live.

Is building a good reputation choice by choice easy? No. But we should never feel defeated, because "The one who is in you is greater than the one who is in the world" (1 John 4:4). God is on our side. Not only that, God is *within* us, giving us the grace and strength to not compromise, even if that means standing alone.

Your choices today will affect your opportunities tomorrow. If you are "sleepy" and checked out, more concerned with having fun and fitting in than with making good choices and building a solid reputation, you will miss all sorts of chances to succeed now and in the future. Your choices are going to affect the way adults see you and the opportunities they will offer you. What are your dreams? Go after them, and identify the poor choices that might get in the way of you achieving them.

Don't waste your life. Don't waste the gift of a good name.

No mistake is beyond the reach of God's mercy and forgiveness, but remember, it's far easier to maintain a good reputation than it is to rebuild a tarnished one.

Discussion Questions:

What are your dreams?

What choices might get in the way of you achieving those dreams?

Is there anything I can be doing to help you go for your dreams?

Quiet your heart. . . .

Ask your daughter for something specific that is on her heart—a dream, a worry, a troubled relationship—and pray for that desire or need.

Dear God,
Help me and [your daughter's name] to not be sleepy or lazy about our choices. May we begin today to build a solid reputation, based on refusing to compromise what we know to be right. We both have a lot of dreams. Help us to pay attention to the choices that might get in the way of us achieving those dreams. Help us to not waste our lives or waste the gift of a good name. We know Your love for us is unconditional, but help us to respond to that love with gratitude and obedience instead of complacency. Thank You for giving us the gift of the Holy Spirit, who always helps us to make the best choices.
Amen.

JOURNALING CONVERSATIONS

Would you rather win an Academy Award, an Olympic medal, or the Nobel Peace Prize?

MOTHER

DAUGHTER

Day 18

AN AUDIENCE OF ONE

We've talked about the importance of not compromising—about making the right decisions even when it's really hard. One of the reasons why it's so difficult to do the right thing, especially when no one else seems to be doing it, is the lie for today: I need the approval of my friends to be happy.

This is one of those lies where there's a little bit of truth in it, so it's easy to believe. The truth is, it's easier to be happy when our friends approve of us. But we don't *need* their approval. And if we only make choices based on what everyone around us thinks, we'll definitely make some wrong decisions.

We're told in 1 Corinthians 16:13–14, "Be on your guard, stand firm in the faith, be courageous, be strong. Your every act should be done with love."

We have to be on our guard, because so many things that lead us down the wrong path look like fun at the beginning. If we aren't paying attention, we'll get sucked into some bad decisions.

We need to stand firm in the faith. More and more as you go through life, you'll encounter people who believe very differently than you do. We are always to respect another person's beliefs, but we are to stand firm in what we know to be true. If we have made people's approval the most important thing to us, then we definitely won't stand firm in the faith; there will just be too many times when doing so will cause us to stand out and look different.

This means that we have to be courageous and strong. Sometimes we'll have to stand alone. And that's OK. In fact, if we *never* find ourselves standing alone, we are probably caving in and compromising.

The last part of that verse says that our every act should be done with love. That means every word we speak is done with love. It means that we are always looking for the farthest person out and determining how we can include her. It means that when we want to sit down and play with our phones or computers, we first look around to see if someone needs help.

Most people don't live like that. But when people do, they change the world.

Pope Benedict XVI challenged us to live that way when he said, "The world offers you comfort. But you were not made for comfort. You were made for greatness."

It takes strength and courage to do this, and it requires that you live for an audience of one. Instead of seeking the approval of your friends and convincing yourself that you need it to be happy, decide that you want to live to make *one* person happy: God.

If, at the end of the day, He is happy with how you have lived and loved, then that is all that matters. And if you mess up, you know what He's like. He will always forgive and give you a fresh start.

We might think that we need friends' approval to be happy, but the truth is found in Nehemiah 8:10: "The joy of the Lord is your strength."

When we live for an audience of *one*, when we live in such a way that we bring God joy, then we are filled with strength. And God never just keeps that joy for Himself; He pours it back into our hearts. Because that's the kind of Father He is.

He's a Father who lavishly loves you, one who keeps His promises. We can count on Him.

Discussion Questions:

What brings you joy?

Who do you think you are trying to please with your decisions? (I know the right answer is God, but who competes for that place in your heart?)

What is your reaction to Pope Benedict XVI's words, "The world offers you comfort. But you were not made for comfort. You were made for greatness"?

Quiet your heart. . . .

Ask your daughter for something specific that is on her heart—a dream, a worry, a troubled relationship—and pray for that desire or need.

Dear God,
Thank You so much for loving us in such a personal way. We are so grateful that You will never, ever leave us. Thank You for Your nonstop, eternal, and never-changing love. Help us to see ourselves through Your eyes. May we see that our words are meaningful to You, that You believe in us, that You created us in such a way that they each bring something unique to the world that no one else can bring. I pray that [your daughter's name] wouldn't change just to fit in, but instead would live as a strong and courageous world changer.
Amen.

JOURNALING CONVERSATIONS

If you could give one million dollars to a charity, which one would you choose?

MOTHER

DAUGHTER

Day 19

TRUE HAPPINESS

Can you think of five things that you believe will make you happy? *[Give your daughter a minute to think of them.]*

If those things came true, would you really be happy forever? Are they all things that are going to last? Are they going to make you happy in the deepest parts of you?

The truth is, many things here on earth bring us temporary happiness, but they don't last. Happiness that truly stays with us forever is called *joy*. We don't get it from our circumstances. It's one of the fruits of the Spirit. We read in Galatians 5:22 that the fruit of the Spirit is love, joy, peace, patience, kindness, goodness, faithfulness, and self-control. This means that when the Holy Spirit fills our hearts, He puts those things within them. That means we have joy as a gift from God. So why don't we feel joy all the time?

Romans 15:13 gives us a hint. It's a prayer written by Saint Paul, who prays, "May the God of hope fill you with all joy and peace as you trust in him."

What do we have to trust God with if we are going to have joy? We have to trust that He actually wants what is best for us—He wants us to have joy, to be fully alive.

Our lie for today:
Following Jesus means I can't have any fun.

Our truth:
"The thief comes only to steal and destroy. I have come that you may have life, and have it to the full." John 10:10

What sounds like so much fun at the beginning is often the enemy coming to steal and destroy. We think we'll get away with something and it'll be great. The enemy, the author of all lies, wants us to think that. He wants us to think the thrill will last forever.

But it doesn't. When we've made a choice that was wrong but fun at the time, we are left with regret and guilt. Our true joy is stolen.

When God tells us that we shouldn't do certain things, it isn't because He's a cosmic killjoy. It's because He knows what will truly bring us an abundant life. He knows what will really make your heart full.

True happiness doesn't come from getting all the things we want or achieving our goals. It actually comes from obeying God.

OBEDIENCE = JOY

To believe that takes trust.

You can decide how you are going to learn this truth. You can learn it the easy way, by trusting God and staying on the path He says is best. Or you can go down another path that might look more fun and try it out. It might be fun for a while. But ultimately, God loves you too much to let you stay on a path that He knows is going to steal your true joy.

When you get caught on that path, I want you to remember something. Being caught is a sign that *God loves you*, that He is pointing you toward something better. It isn't the end of the world; it isn't the end of the road. It's one of the ways He offers you a fresh start. But you will be learning the hard way that OBEDIENCE = JOY.

It's my prayer for you that you would trust God's plan and stay on the path He says is best. When we follow His plan, we discover the things that will make us happy forever, not just temporarily. Saint John Paul II says it so well: "It is Jesus that you seek when you dream of happiness; He is waiting for you when nothing else you find satisfies you."

Jesus and His plan for your life are the source of true happiness. The saints knew this. In fact, Saint Augustine said, "Learn to dance, or else the angels in heaven will not know what to do with you." God is not a cosmic killjoy; He is the one who knows best what will truly make you happy.

There's obedience in terms of what we do and obedience in terms of what we think. What we think is going to impact what we do. Thoughts motivate and influence behavior.

During our conversations, we've been talking about truth versus lies. Following the truth is going to bring us joy. Believing the lies will take us down the path where we learn things the hard way. The choice is ours.

Discussion Questions:

How would you describe the difference between happiness and joy?

What difficult choices are you facing right now?

What do you think heaven will be like?

Quiet your heart. . . .

Ask your daughter for something specific that is on her heart—a dream, a worry, a troubled relationship—and pray for that desire or need.

Dear God,
I pray that [your daughter's name] would be wide open to the truth that You are not holding out on her, trying to spoil her fun. May she know and believe that You know, even better than she does, what will truly bring her lasting joy. I pray that she would grow in maturity so that she can see that the guidelines You give us are to keep us safe. You came to earth so that we could have an abundant life. Your rules are for our protection, not our destruction. I pray that this precious girl would learn life's lessons the easy way, but for the times when the hard way is chosen, I pray that she would know that there is always a road home to You. You always meet us with mercy. Thank You for Your unconditional love.
Amen.

JOURNALING CONVERSATIONS

MOTHER: Write a message to your younger self.

DAUGHTER: Write a message to your future self.

Day 20

YOU CHOOSE

"We can choose a path that leads us into trouble. It all comes down to our decisions at the end of the day." —Olympic athlete Gabby Douglas

Have you ever worried that your worst decision or most embarrassing moment is going to follow you forever? The truth is, our choices have consequences. God always forgives, but it sometimes takes people a long time to forget. This is why it's so important that we learn to be good decision makers.

Your reputation has everything to do with the choices you make, which means it's critical that you become a good decision maker. It's been said that reputation is built through commitment and self-discipline. You commit to not compromising in certain areas, and then you stay self-disciplined even if making the right choice is hard and costs you a friendship.

Sometimes we think that we are defined by one big choice. That was the case for a girl named Jana. Jana was a good enough student, a great athlete, and really well liked. One night in high school, she went to a party with underage drinking and the police showed up. Jana hadn't been drinking, but simply because she was at the party, she was put into a police car along with the others and briefly spent time in jail. She was traumatized by the experience, and felt that this was just one really bad decision that she'd made. But is this really true? Was she in that situation because of just one bad decision?

Jana had made the decision to choose friends who drank in high school.
Jana had made the decision to straddle the fence, never taking a stand for what was right and wrong. Her goal was just to fit in.
Jana had made the decision to go to a party that served alcohol to underage kids.
Jana had made the decision to stay at the party.
Jana had made the decision to care more about what her friends thought than what was legal.
All her little choices mattered.

Alexa is an incredible athlete, playing lacrosse for a well-known Division I college. She gets good grades and is set up to have a great career after she graduates at the top of her class. She's got true friends and knows who she is.

Alexa made the decision to study hard in high school.
Alexa made the decision to choose friends who brought out the best in her, not the ones who tried to get her to compromise.
Alexa made the decision to work hard at her sport instead of hurting her body with alcohol.
Alexa made the decision to push herself to excel instead of always taking the easy way out.
Alexa made the decision to spend time each day reading her Bible and praying. This helped her to remember who she was—God's beloved daughter.
Alexa made the decision to care more about what God thought about her than what the kids in her class thought.

What we think are small decisions actually build on one another and shape what kind of big decisions we make later on.

Your good choices need to be *consistent*. That way you become known as a person of good character. Your reputation will cause people to give you the benefit of the doubt. But if you're known as a person who doesn't respect adults or breaks the rules, people will assume the worst. This won't always seem fair. But it's the result of whichever choices you make consistently.

Our choices matter—not just the big ones, but the little ones, too. That's all truth.

So what's our lie for today? It grows out of the times when our choices aren't so great. As much as I want you to choose the easy path, the one filled with the right choices, I know how hard this is. I know that we aren't perfect. I'm not; you're not. So there are going to be times when we fail.

Some of those failures will be private, and most people won't know about them. Some of them might be public, which is a lot harder.

Our lie for today:
My reputation will always follow me.

This is a powerful lie, because there is a little bit of truth to it. People will remember when you fall. Not everyone will be gracious to you about it. But you are not defined by other people's opinions of you. And regardless of what it might feel like, there is always the opportunity for a fresh start.

The truth is found in 2 Corinthians 5:17: "If anyone is in Christ, he is a new creation. The old has gone. The new has come."

With God, there is always a second chance, a fresh start. Always. As Saint Augustine said, "There's no saint without a past, and no sinner without a future." The truth is, your choices matter. And equally true: You always have a chance at a fresh start with God.

And when He forgives, He throws your sin as far as the east is from the west (Psalm 103:12).

It's really important that you believe this, because otherwise when you make a mistake, you'll likely try to hide it, or try to figure it out for yourself. But it's always better to bring things into the light and involve an adult. We are for you. We want what is best for you. Anything you face will be faced better with the help of an adult who loves you.

Discussion Questions:

Do you want to chart a new course?

What kind of a reputation do you want to have?

What do you think is a great way to make a fresh start with God?

Quiet your heart. . . .

Ask your daughter for something specific that is on her heart—a dream, a worry, a troubled relationship—and pray for that desire or need.

Dear God,
Help us to understand the importance of all our small choices and the way they lead us to big decisions. Give us wisdom so that we recognize the right path to take. Help us to choose our friends wisely, because we know how much they will influence our choices. And for those times when we make mistakes, may we remember that with You, there is always a second chance. You always offer a fresh start. May we run to You for

mercy instead of trying to hide or figure things out for ourselves. Help us to know and believe that it's always better to bring things into the light.
Amen.

JOURNALING CONVERSATIONS

MOTHER: When I was your age, I wanted to grow up to be . . .

DAUGHTER: When I grow up, I want to be . . .

NOTES

Day 21

GOD IS CALLING YOUR NAME

"The Lord your God is in your midst, a mighty savior, who will rejoice over you with gladness, and renew you in his love, who will sing joyfully because of you."
Zephaniah 3:17

God is so excited about you. He made you in His image and likeness and He wants you to know that He would do absolutely anything for you. He loves you more than you can possibly imagine. He died for you. Because you are so amazing in His eyes, He rejoices and sings over you.

There is a wonderful camp in the mountains of Georgia called Covecrest, and every Monday night during the summer, around two hundred teens run through an obstacle course. At the end of the course, they are completely covered in mud from head to toe. Sometimes they even end up bleeding and bruised and so dirty they can't even see the color of their own skin.

And yet, every Monday night, week after week, Jesus meets every teen at camp in his or her mess, right where they are. He is carried across the field to meet them in the sacrament of the Eucharist at adoration. For many of the teens, it's the most impactful time of the camp experience, a powerful reminder that God doesn't require us to be perfect. He comes to us in our brokenness and imperfection.

How often do you feel too messy to be loved by God? Do you ever feel broken, imperfect, or ashamed before Jesus?

Well, stop right there, because Jesus sees your mess and He loves you anyway. He sees your brokenness and He calls you His beloved daughter. When you are covered in mud, He wraps you in His embrace. There is absolutely nothing you can do to make Jesus love you any more or any less. So, despite your imperfections, invite Him to remind you of how much you are worth.

I'd like you to close your eyes as I speak some truths, some blessings, over you.

You are God's beloved daughter.
You are a princess because you are a daughter of the King.
You are priceless.
You are beautiful.
You are a unique, one-of-a-kind daughter of God.
There is no one else in this world like you and He is crazy about you.

Each day, I pray you would wake up and remember these words. Ask God to help convince your heart that in Him, *you are enough.* There is no one else in this world like you and that fact is amazing. Let Jesus love you in your mess. Hear His words. You are the beloved!

God has a unique plan for your life, and the moment you start comparing yourself to others, you risk missing out on this one-of-a-kind plan.

Remember the words of Saint Catherine of Siena? "Be who God meant you to be and you will set the world on fire." When you recognize and embrace your unique belovedness, you have the opportunity to set the world on fire.

If you're wondering just how much you can do at your age, remember that Saint Maria Goretti was only twelve years old when she died. She was the age of a middle-schooler, yet she set the world on fire with her love for God. She fulfilled her unique role in life and became a saint before she was even a teenager.

Where Maria Goretti grew up, she and her family shared a small house with another farm worker, Giovanni Serenelli, and his twenty-year-old son, Alessandro. Giovanni tried to drown his anger in drink, and Maria and her mother froze in fear whenever he would enter the building drunk, cursing, throwing things, and banging into the walls and doors. But they feared Alessandro even more. Giovanni flared up in hot temper, but Alessandro nursed a cold anger that ran deep, corrupting his heart.

It was the anger inside Alessandro that made him do it—anger and hatred, resentment for the misery of his life spent ankle-deep in marshland mud, fury at the hopelessness of his future, frustration at having dreams and desires unmet. Maria was doing her needlework in the house when Alessandro swept in and attacked her. She tried to reason with him, telling him that what he was doing was a mortal sin, but something inside him broke. Alessandro unleashed his fury and killed her, stabbing her fourteen times.

Even as she was dying, Maria entrusted herself to God and the Blessed Virgin Mary. She prayed to be found, prayed for Alessandro, prayed for her mother, and prayed for God to accept her soul. By the grace of God, she chose to forgive.

After her death, God permitted Maria to appear to Alessandro in a dream, bearing fourteen white lilies in her arms. He had walled himself off from everyone for three years, refusing to communicate—unrepentant, locked in the interior prison of his own anger, unable to forgive himself. Maria presented him with the white lilies—her pardon—and when he reached out to take them, they turned into flames that burned his hands. She said to him, "Alessandro, it is time to let go of the anger that burns you inside, making your soul a blackened wasteland, sterile and hard. It is time to let forgiveness wash through you like a river; time to let God turn your desert into green, healthy land. It is time to be made new." He listened, and by a special grace, he was healed. In accepting Maria's forgiveness, he also learned to forgive; he learned to let go of the darkness he had been clinging to so tightly.

Alessandro and Maria's mother were reconciled, and he eventually became a lay brother with the Order of Friars Minor Capuchin. There he worked as a receptionist, welcoming people in, and as a gardener, making green things grow. Alessandro was healed, and twenty years after witnessing Maria Goretti's canonization in 1950, he died of old age, in peace. He had come a long way from the malaria fields to the Good Shepherd's fold.

Do you ever think that you can't make a difference in the world by the way you speak, live, and love because of your young age? Well that, my sweet daughter, is a lie. The Bible clearly states that your age has nothing to do with the difference you can make. And if the Bible says so, it must be true. Because the Bible only speaks the truth, and we will find that out over and over again as we continue through these readings together.

Discussion Questions:

What is something unique about you?

How does it make you feel to think of God singing over you?

What did you learn from the story of Saint Maria Goretti?

Quiet your heart. . . .

Ask your daughter for something specific that is on her heart—a dream, a worry, a troubled relationship—and pray for that desire or need.

Dear God,
Help [your daughter's name] dream big about the difference she can make in the world. Give her the passion and the focus to start bringing change right where she is. Instead of believing the lie that she is too young to make a difference, may she look for opportunities to love and forgive wherever she finds herself. When she encounters a situation that makes it hard to forgive, may she ask You to fill her with divine love. May You do in and through her what she feels is impossible. May she rely utterly on You and the power of the Holy Spirit.
Amen.

JOURNALING CONVERSATIONS

What is an accomplishment you are proud of?

MOTHER

DAUGHTER

NOTES

Day 22

COUNTERING THE LIES

Whether you realize it or not, you are constantly bombarded with messages and images from the media and the culture, hitting you with lie after lie.

One of the main lies girls face today is the one that says in order to be loved, you have to meet a certain standard of beauty. Today that standard seems to be something along the lines of: size 0 with tight abs, golden skin, and a clear complexion with a perfectly carefree smile at all times.

What messages do you think are being communicated by the media and the culture?
[Let your daughter answer.]

What does it do to your body image?
[Let your daughter answer.]

Do you think any of those messages are actually lies?
[Let your daughter answer.]

Our culture says a lot to girls. Some of these lies include:

You should always look happy.
You should be stick-thin.
You should be athletic.

This culture holds girls to an unbelievably high standard. It only makes sense that girls today are riddled with body image issues.

What are some of the messages that counter these lies?
[Let your daughter answer.]

It's OK to be real. It's OK to be you. It doesn't matter if you're curvy or thin. It doesn't matter if you have freckles or a clear face. You are beautiful just the way you are. But these truths are sometimes hard to believe. It can be difficult to distinguish the truth from the lies. Lies are always louder than the truth, and most people believe the lies. But Archbishop Fulton J. Sheen warned people about this: "The truth is the truth even if no one believes it, and a lie is a lie even if everyone believes it."

So what are we supposed to do? Instead of just accepting things at face value, we need to slow down and ask ourselves if what we are hearing or seeing is what God would say. We hold what we've heard up to the light of what we know of God. We examine things before we believe them.

We're told in the Bible that Jesus is the light of the world (John 8:12). His voice in the Bible can act as a light when we are trying to figure out what is true and what's a lie. In verse John 14:6, Jesus is described as "the way, and the truth, and the life." This means we can trust Jesus because He only speaks the truth. As we get to know Him—as we come to recognize His voice—we'll be able to recognize the difference between truth and lies.

So how do we do that? How do we grow in our ability to recognize the voice of Jesus? We go to the place where we find His words: the Bible. This is where we turn when we want to recognize truth.

The Bible speaks the ultimate truth, and we need to compare every lie we hear to what we read in those pages.

For example, when the world tells us that in order to be beautiful and loved we have to meet a certain standard of outward beauty, the Bible tells us, "Charm is deceptive and beauty fleeting; the woman who fears the Lord is to be praised" (Proverbs 31:30). This means the things the world says matter most—being charming and beautiful on the outside—can't be counted on. They're not what is most important. What God says matters most is that we fear the Lord. This doesn't mean we're afraid of Him; it means we respect Him and acknowledge that His opinion is the one that matters most.

We can't prevent lies from intersecting our thoughts. Every day you will hear different things that you will be tempted to believe as the truth. But you can choose to reject the lies and turn to the truth found in Scripture instead.

When we study the truth found in Scripture and in our Catholic faith and we dwell on what is true about us and about others, we are going to recognize the things that are false. We will be stronger, empowered, and happier as a result!

Discussion Questions:

Where do you go when you need to know the truth about something? Who do you ask? What websites do you turn to?

Do you believe that truth is found in the Bible?

Quiet your heart. . . .

Ask your daughter for something specific that is on her heart—a dream, a worry, a troubled relationship—and pray for that desire or need.

Dear God,
Fill our hearts with Your truth. Grant us the wisdom to know Your voice and choose Your truths over the lies of this world. God, we believe in Your goodness and we believe that Your words are greater than this world. Give us the discernment that we need to put what we have learned today into practice. Lord, You are good. Thank You for Your truth.
Amen.

JOURNALING CONVERSATIONS

If you could travel anywhere in the world, where would you go and why?

MOTHER

DAUGHTER

Day 23

THE BIBLE IS A GIFT

During our conversations, we have talked about your identity as God's beloved daughter. We've discussed the reality that you have a unique role to fulfill in life and that, despite your age, you can make a difference in the world *today*. We've been exploring the concept of truth versus lies; we've learned that there are a lot of lies that we face every day, and often these lies can disguise themselves as the truth quite well. Because of this, it is important to get to know the voice of God and be able to hear His truth over the lies of this world.

Every time you go to Mass, you face the lie that the Bible has nothing significant to say to you today. You hear a reading from the Old Testament, a reading from the New Testament, and a Gospel reading. Often the passages seem to be speaking to a group of people on another planet. Sometimes the stories are at the very least familiar, although there's always that rare occasion when the readings surprisingly relate to something going on in your life at the time.

The truth is that although the Bible may seem outdated and useless, it has a lot to say to you. The Bible is the main way Jesus speaks to you. Reading it is one of the best ways to come to hear and know the truth-speaking voice of God. The Bible is where you can come to know your identity as the beloved daughter of a loving King, where you can learn how God is calling you to set the world on fire.

I hope that you'll be willing to come to the Bible with your questions, because God truly does have the answers to the things you worry about. Let's take a look at the Virgin Mary to see what I mean. In Luke 1:26–38, Mary was about your age.

You have probably often heard of this story as the Annunciation. In it we learn that an angel, Gabriel, appeared to Mary. He greeted her and informed her that he was speaking God's words, and then he told her that she was going to become pregnant and have a baby. This wasn't just any baby, but the Son of God.

Imagine someone telling you that on a random afternoon!

In this moment, I imagine Mary faced many lies:

This is impossible. I'm a virgin!
This is not what I'm supposed to do. I'm supposed to marry Joseph.
Joseph will leave me because he will think that I cheated on him.
Everyone will hate me if I have a child outside of marriage.

I'm sure every one of these lies (and many more) went through Mary's head on that day. And yet she chose to hear the voice of God—the voice of truth—among the lies and said yes to what God was calling her to do. By saying yes to God, Mary set the world on fire.

We learn from Luke 1:46–55 that Mary knew Holy Scripture. Her famous prayer from that passage is called the Magnificat:

> My soul proclaims the greatness of the Lord, my spirit rejoices in God my Savior, for he has looked with favor on his lowly servant. From this day all generations will call me blessed; the Almighty has done great things for me, and holy is his Name. He has mercy on those who fear him in every generation. He has shown the strength of his arm, he has scattered the proud in their conceit. He has cast down the mighty from their thrones, and has lifted up the lowly. He has filled the hungry with good things, and the rich he has sent away empty. He has come to the help of his servant Israel for he remembered his promise of mercy, the promise he made to our fathers, to Abraham and his children forever.

What many people don't realize is that the truths contained in her prayer are based on many Old Testament passages.[6] The Blessed Mother knew who she was and, most important, whose she was. This knowledge, combined with all she knew of her faith, helped her to resist the lies that swirled around her and to keep her eye on what God had called her to do.

You may not have an angel standing in front of you when you are facing lies, but the Bible is your angel Gabriel. It will respond to those lies and announce to you the good news of Jesus Christ. The Bible will affirm your identity and challenge you to respond to what God is calling you to do. The Bible is your ultimate source of truth. Will you choose to listen to what it says?

---

[6] 1 Sam. 2:1; Isa. 61:10; Hab. 3:18; Ps. 25:2, 145:6, 28:7; 1 Sam. 1:11; Gen. 30:13; Ps. 103:1, 105:3, 111:9, 145:21; 103:17, 89:11, 113:7–8; Job 5:11, 12:19; Ps. 107:41, 113:7–8; 1 Sam. 2:8, 2:4; Isa. 40:29; Ps. 107:9; 1 Sam. 2:5; Isa. 41:8–9; Ps. 98:3; Gen. 12:3, 13:15, 22:16–18, 26:3–4, 28:13–14; Lev. 26:42; Deut. 1:8, 6:10, 9:5, 25, 27; Sir. 44:19; Mic. 7:20, Ps. 105:8–10

Every truth is followed by at least a dozen lies close behind it. And sometimes, these lies catch up with you and make it hard to see the truth. That is why it is important to closely examine everything you are told is true and see if the Bible agrees. If Scripture backs up what you're questioning, it's true. If it doesn't, it's a lie. Seek out truth in the words of Jesus.

We will continue to do this together until understanding the truth of Jesus becomes second nature to us. Until then, I want to act as your angel Gabriel for the day.

Greetings! You are God's beloved daughter and He is so incredibly pleased with you! I have good news: God has sent me to challenge you to dive deeper into Scripture every single day. He wants you to know His words because He has a beautiful plan for your life. Keep listening to what He has to say!

Discussion Questions:

What did you think of the Bible before we began these readings together? Do you look at it differently now?

Would you be willing to start reading a little bit of the Bible each day, following Mary's example of knowing her faith well?

Quiet your heart. . . .

Ask your daughter for something specific that is on her heart—a dream, a worry, a troubled relationship—and pray for that desire or need.

Dear God,
Thank You for giving us the example of the Blessed Mother. Her trust in You wasn't just blind trust—it came after years of faithfully getting to know You. Help us to become more like her. Give us a hunger to know Your truth and the willingness to study in order to be equipped to fight the lies in the world. May we turn to You for truth instead of to the internet or people. We can find good information in so many places, but help us to turn to You first.
Amen.

JOURNALING CONVERSATIONS

What do you wish you could do more often?

MOTHER

DAUGHTER

Day 24

MORE THAN ENOUGH

The world constantly tells us what we are not rather than what we are.

You are not pretty enough.
Your hair is not straight enough.
You're not tan enough.
You're not thin enough.
You're not smart enough.
You're not athletic enough.

I could go on; the list of "not enoughs" seems endless.

Take Instagram, for example. You assume that if you get a certain number of likes on your posts, you will suddenly be enough. You probably sit on social media for hours at a time scrolling through other girls' feeds, comparing yourself to them. You likely sit in class comparing yourself to others rather than recognizing your own unique beauty.

Do you know what is going on below the surface? You are being robbed. Something is being taken from you in those moments of comparison, and it's one of the things that make life worth living. It's been said that comparison is the thief of joy, so why can't we stop? Sometimes comparison motivates us, but most of the time it makes us miserable. Let's try to look at ourselves through the eyes of God so we can reclaim our joy.

Jesus liked you before social media even existed. In the story of creation found in Genesis 1, we hear that He looked at you, His creation, and saw that you were good. He was pleased with you from the beginning. He affirmed your identity and beauty before anyone else even knew what you would look like. In His eyes, you are good no matter what. This is the lesson we learn from Genesis 2:18–23:

> The LORD God said: It is not good for the man to be alone. I will make a helper suited to him. So the LORD God formed out of the ground all the wild animals

> and all the birds of the air, and he brought them to the man to see what he would call them; whatever the man called each living creature was then its name. The man gave names to all the tame animals, all the birds of the air, and all the wild animals; but none proved to be a helper suited to the man. So the LORD God cast a deep sleep on the man, and while he was asleep, he took out one of his ribs and closed up its place with flesh. The LORD God then built the rib that he had taken from the man into a woman. When he brought her to the man, the man said:
>
> "This one, at last, is bone of my bones and flesh of my flesh;
> This one shall be called 'woman,' for out of man this one has been taken."

I want you to focus on that last verse. Woman was the last piece of creation made by God. Women—you and I—are the crowning jewel of creation. We are the grand finale. We are God's finishing touch. He could not top what He had made when He created women, so He finished creating. Nothing in all of creation is more beautiful or more special than woman. The most beautiful sunrise is not as beautiful as you. And yet, women are plagued with feelings of not being good enough.

There was a girl named Maddie, the most beautiful girl in school by far. Everyone knew it. Then she started modeling—and everything changed. She was no longer happy with her appearance. She started comparing herself to everyone else she was modeling with and she suddenly wanted to be thinner, fitter, blonder, prettier.

Before long she started taking diet pills, whitening her teeth nightly, bleaching her hair, and fake-tanning weekly. The modeling industry called her to be more, better, perfect. She was beautiful and yet she had lost sight of her beauty. And the more she modeled and was told she was beautiful, the more she forgot that beauty.

This is what social media does. Instagram pictures are posted at specific times to ensure the maximum number of likes. Captions go through several drafts before making the final cut. And the affirming comments that end up under pictures make everyone want to post an even better picture next time.

When Maddie started modeling, instead of feeling great about the opportunity, she felt pressure to be *more* beautiful. She no longer stood out– there was always someone to compare herself to, and she constantly felt the need to be more. Does comparison ever have this effect on you? Do you ever feel pressure to be more–to look better?

Today, I want to challenge you to remember that *you are more than enough.*

Saint Augustine reminds us, "Since love grows within you, so beauty grows. For love is the beauty of the soul." Striving for beauty does not make you more beautiful. Love is the only thing that strengthens beauty—so love yourself. Love one another. Affirm your friends not so that they will affirm you back but so they will experience authentic love. Affirm your friends for the way they love, not the way they look. Only giving and receiving love in this way will allow beauty to flourish.

So acknowledge the lie that your worth is connected to how many likes and comments you get on social media, and hold tight to the truth that you are the absolute crown of creation—you are the most beautiful piece created by God. Don't let comparison rob you of joy.

Discussion Questions:

Who do you compare yourself to most often on social media?

Who do you compare yourself to most often at school?

What are some ways that you love well?

Quiet your heart. . . .

Ask your daughter for something specific that is on her heart—a dream, a worry, a troubled relationship—and pray for that desire or need.

Dear God,
Thank You for making women the crown of creation. When we start to focus on all the things we don't like about our appearance, help us to remember that You consider us more beautiful than a sunset. May our focus shift away from measuring beauty on the outside and instead turn to how we love. May we love well and affirm others for the way they love, not how they look.
Amen.

JOURNALING CONVERSATIONS

What is your favorite sport to play? (Or if you don't like sports, why?) How do sports make you feel about your body?

MOTHER

DAUGHTER

Day 25

BEAUTY OF THE SOUL

If you were to describe to a stranger what Jesus looks like, what would you say? *[Let your daughter answer.]*

Listen to how Josephus, a Jewish historian, described Jesus:

> Both his nature and his form were human: for he was a man of simple appearance, mature age, short growth, three cubits tall [about four and a half feet, based on the Jewish cubit], with scanty hair, but having a line in the middle of the head after the fashion of the Naziraeans, eyebrows meeting above the nose so that the spectators could take fright, with a long face, a long nose, and with an undeveloped beard, dark skin, and hunchbacked.[7]

Does this supposed description of Jesus change your opinion of Him? Do you now think less of Him because He could have been ugly by our standards today? Does Jesus' physical appearance affect His beauty?

My guess is probably not. My guess is that no matter what Jesus looked like, you would love Him just the same. I would imagine you agree that despite His physical appearance, it is His inward self that makes Him beautiful. Jesus is not popular because He had great hair, the best clothes, and perfect skin. He is popular because He loves you so much that He died for you. He is popular because of *who* He is, not because of *what* He looked like.

The world tells you that what makes a person beautiful is clear skin, a perfect body, great hair, and cute clothes. This is a lie.

---

[7] Robert Eisler, *Messiah Jesus and John the Baptist According to Flavius Josephus* (New York: Dial Press, 1931), 425–29.

Proverbs 31:10–30 gives us a description of a beautiful woman:

Who can find a woman of worth?
Far beyond jewels is her value. . . .
She picks out a field and acquires it;
from her earnings she plants a vineyard.
She girds herself with strength;
she exerts her arms with vigor.
She enjoys the profit from her dealings;
her lamp is never extinguished at night.
She puts her hands to the distaff,
and her fingers ply the spindle.
She reaches out her hands to the poor,
and extends her arms to the needy.
She is not concerned for her household when it snows—
all her charges are doubly clothed.
She makes her own coverlets;
fine linen and purple are her clothing. . . .
She makes garments and sells them,
and stocks the merchants with belts.
She is clothed with strength and dignity,
and laughs at the days to come.
She opens her mouth in wisdom;
kindly instruction is on her tongue.
She watches over the affairs of her household,
and does not eat the bread of idleness.
Her children rise up and call her blessed;
her husband, too, praises her:
"Many are the women of proven worth,
but you have excelled them all."
Charm is deceptive and beauty fleeting;
the woman who fears the LORD is to be praised.

Verse 30 reminds us that charm can be misleading, and physical beauty fades. The women who are truly worthy of admiration are those who fear God. This doesn't mean that we are supposed to be afraid of Him—it's a phrase used to describe a woman who honors and respects God and gives Him first priority in her life. That is true inner beauty, and it lasts.

Physical beauty is temporary at best. A woman is beautiful, therefore, not because she is by definition "pretty"; she is beautiful because, as Scripture tells us, she is strong (Proverbs 31:17), generous (31:20), hardworking (31:24), wise (31:26), and full of joy (31:28), and she loves God above all else (31:30).

What makes a woman beautiful is not clear skin, a perfect body, great hair, or cute clothes. What makes a woman beautiful is the light of God radiating from her.

Venerable Archbishop Fulton J. Sheen shares his wisdom on this topic, writing, "Beauty on the outside never gets into the soul, but beauty of the soul reflects itself on the face."

People spend a lot of time and money working on their exterior appearance, but they forget that it takes a lot of time and energy to work on their interior appearance. Jesus was beautiful no matter what He actually looked like because His soul was reflected in His face. I can only imagine how much beauty we would see if we all recognized this truth—that it is what our *souls* look like that truly matters.

Think about Saint Teresa of Calcutta. You have probably more often heard her referred to as Mother Teresa because she just became a saint in 2016 (that's right, this great saint was canonized in *your* lifetime). This amazing woman of God devoted her entire life to serving and loving the poorest of the poor in Calcutta, India. She cared for the sick and the dying, the disabled, the orphaned, and everyone in between. Despite every difficulty or uncertainty she faced, she loved God and continually said yes to His plan for her life.

Yet if you showed a picture of her to a group of people who had no idea who she was or how she lived her life, they would be unlikely to say that she was pretty. Her skin was wrinkled from long days in the sun. Her eyes were sunken in from hours upon hours of labor. And I would imagine that the hair beneath her white-and-blue habit (the garment worn on her head) was gray. She was an old woman who had not aged well by society's standards.

And yet, she was voted the most admired person of the twentieth century. People were fascinated by the beauty they saw in her. They were absolutely drawn to her.

Saint John Paul II described her this way: "It is not surprising that the people of our time were fascinated by her. She incarnated that love which Jesus indicated as the distinctive mark of disciples: 'By this all men will know that you are my disciples, if you have love for one another' (John 13:35)."[8]

People were not fascinated by and drawn to Mother Teresa because of her physical beauty, but because of the inner beauty that flowed from the way she loved. Mother Teresa radiated joy, which she described as a "net of love." There was beauty in her smile, love was in her eyes, and her lifetime of service was expressed in her wrinkles. It is clear that she lived a life of love.

---

[8] The Holy See, "Address of the Holy Father John Paul II To the Meeting of the Adoptive Families Organized by the Missionaries of Charity," http://w2.vatican.va/content/john-paul-ii/en/speeches/2000/jul-sep/documents/hf_jp-ii_spe_20000905_adozioni.html, accessed May 3, 2018.

Mother Teresa easily could have said no to God and lived a different life. She could have spent her time and money in keeping up her physical appearance. She could have used a variety of face creams to avoid such excessive wrinkling. She could have worn makeup to cover up her imperfections. She could have had cosmetic surgery to tighten her face. She could have dyed her hair. . . . She could have done a lot of things to make herself more beautiful based on the standards of this world.

Yet Mother Teresa chose to embrace the way she had been created by God. She chose to love her flaws and imperfections, and she changed the world by doing so.

Mother Teresa was beautiful despite the fact that she did not have perfect skin, a perfect body, great hair, or cute clothes. She was beautiful with her wrinkled skin, shriveled body, hidden hair, and blue-and-white uniform.

This woman transformed the world by recognizing what we read today in the book of Proverbs—that beauty is fleeting but a woman who loves the Lord is to be admired. Mother Teresa was most certainly admired.

When you begin to doubt your appearance and compare yourself to others, stop. Look instead at women like Mother Teresa. God wants us to focus on our hearts more than our physical appearances. He wants us to focus on the way we love more than we focus on the way we look. I challenge you to do this next time insecurities well up inside you.

Because as a good friend constantly reminds me, "Smile! God loves you even on a bad hair day!"

Discussion Questions:

What are some ways you can focus on your heart more than your physical appearance?

What things compete with God for first place in your heart?

Archbishop Fulton Sheen said, "Beauty on the outside never gets into the soul, but beauty of the soul reflects itself on the face." Have you ever seen this in a woman you have encountered?

Quiet your heart. . . .

Ask your daughter for something specific that is on her heart—a dream, a worry, a troubled relationship—and pray for that desire or need.

Dear God,
Help us to look at ourselves through your eyes. Instead of focusing on our physical appearances, may we remember that it's our souls that truly matter. When our souls are filled with joy, gratitude and love, that beauty overflows and actually makes us look radiant on the outside. May that be our focus– may we cultivate the habits of being thankful, thinking of others, and doing what we can to actively love those around us.
Amen.

JOURNALING CONVERSATIONS

Which woman do you most admire for her inner beauty?

MOTHER

DAUGHTER

Day 26

THE UNCONDITIONAL LOVE OF GOD

"Authentic love transforms the human person." —Sister Miriam Heidland, SOLT

Sr. Miriam James Heidland was a girl much like you. She grew up Catholic, was bored to tears, went to church every Sunday, and learned a lot of rules.[9] She was super athletic and absolutely loved volleyball. In fact, she loved it so much that she went on to play for a Division I team in college.

And yet, in reflecting on her time as a young girl she says, "I didn't see or understand God as my loving Father who watches over me and speaks to me in my heart. I saw him as the 'policeman in the sky' who notes everything I do wrong and who was overwhelmingly disappointed with me . . ."[10] She didn't know that God loved her no matter what. She hadn't fallen in love with Christ; she'd never had a personal encounter with Him.

You see, despite her seemingly perfect appearance, Sr. Miriam also really struggled to feel satisfied and loved. She dated many guys and dressed immodestly to get their attention.[11] And she constantly compared herself to all the girls around her. She partied and drank a lot. In fact, she was an alcoholic by the time she was twenty-one.[12]

She fought with her parents a lot. She disrespected them and constantly rebelled against and lied to her mother. She suffered from depression and spent a lot of time feeling worthless and unloved.[13] There were secrets she held close to her chest—of abuse as a child, of her addiction to alcohol; part of her hated her life. She assumed God couldn't love her because of the things that had happened to her.

But a couple of people loved her in such a way that it broke through all the barriers. A priest began to tell her the truth about God and about how precious she was to Him.

---

[9] Miriam James Heidland, SOLT, *Loved as I Am* (Notre Dame, IN: Ave Maria Press, 2014), 9–10.
[10] Ibid., 10.
[11] Ibid., 16.
[12] Ibid., 45.
[13] Ibid., 48.

He was a witness of holiness; there was something captivating about His life. She didn't know exactly what it was, but she knew she wanted it.

At the same time, her mother, having reached a point of desperation, got on her knees and gave her away to the Blessed Mother. She began to fast and pray that her daughter would become a nun. After countless prayers, many years, and deep struggles, her daughter came to really *know* God—not as the "policeman in the sky" but as the man who loves her unconditionally.

In her book, *Loved as I Am*, Sr. Miriam reflects on this new understanding: "We are very good because we are created in the image and likeness of God who is goodness mimself. We can know and love because God knows and loves. The *best* of our knowing and loving here on earth is only a splinter of the perfection of how God knows and loves eternally. He made us, we belong to him, and we long for him whether we realize it or not."[14]

When we think about our identities—for example, if someone asks, "Who are you?"—it is often easy to describe ourselves with the things we do. We're also quick to describe ourselves based on our achievements. But when we base our identity on those things, we become insecure, because they can all be gone in an instant.

God has given you a different identity. And you did not have to do a thing to receive it. He calls you His beloved daughter. He tells you that you are loved by Him. He wants you to root your identity in the reality that He "so loved the world that he gave his one and only Son, that whoever believes in him shall not perish but have eternal life. For God did not send his Son into the world to condemn the world, but to save the world through him" (John 3:16–17).

God is the opposite of the "policeman in the sky." He does not keep a record of all that you have done. He simply loves you. He does not condemn you; He saves you.

You live in a world that expects you to achieve. Your coaches expect you to be the best athlete you can be. Your teachers expect you to get A's. Your faith formation teachers expect you to follow God unfailingly in all you do. And your parents expect you to do as much as you can and the best you can to prepare for the next step in life.

Today's lie: My identity is found in earthly achievements.
Today's truth: Your identity is as a beloved daughter of God.

[14] Ibid., 8.

The Bible confirms this truth when Saint Paul tells us, "For I am convinced that neither death, nor life, nor angels, nor principalities, nor things present, nor things to come, nor powers, nor height, nor depth, nor any other created thing, will be able to separate us from the love of God, which is in Christ Jesus our Lord" (Romans 8:38–39).

This means nothing can stand between you and God. He loves you no matter what.

But don't worry if you're still not convinced. Even saints need to be reminded of this truth. In a vision, Saint Teresa of Ávila once heard Jesus say to her, "I would create the world again just to hear you say, 'I love you.'"

Jesus created the entire world for you. Before you had the opportunity to claim your identity or prove yourself to be a "good person," God gave you the greatest gift anyone has ever received. Your past actions did not encourage Him to do this, nor do your present and future actions affirm God in His actions or make Him regret giving you such a beautiful gift. God created the whole world for you. He died for you. And He did all of that just to hear you tell Him that you love Him.

God wakes you up every morning with a stunning sunrise for one reason—He wants to tell you that He loves you. And every night, the day ends with a magnificent sunset because He wants you to fall asleep knowing that you are loved.

He wants to say to you, "My daughter, know you are my beloved. Know that I am well pleased with you. Know that nothing you do or say can change my opinion of you. Know that to be a Christian does not mean that you have to be a 'good person.' To be a Christian is a gift. And it simply means that you know you are loved by me, the creator of the universe. Allow me to love you each and every day. Hear me saying, 'I love you.'"

I pray that you would go forth knowing that truth today.

Discussion Questions:

Can you think of any secret a girl might hold close to her chest, worried that people won't love her if the secret is known?

What do you think God would say to her as she holds her secret close?

If someone were to ask you, "Who are you?" what would you say? Which accomplishments or abilities would spring to your mind?

Quiet your heart. . . .

Ask your daughter for something specific that is on her heart—a dream, a worry, a troubled relationship—and pray for that desire or need.

Dear God,
Help us to hear Your voice calling us the beloved. May we truly believe that there is no secret that we should withhold from You. May we truly believe that there is nothing that could happen to us or that we could do that would cause You to withdraw Your love. Help us to know You as our compassionate, unconditionally loving Father.
Amen.

JOURNALING CONVERSATIONS

Things I find easy to talk to you about:
Things that are hard to talk about:

MOTHER

DAUGHTER

NOTES

Day 27

YOUR HEART'S DESIRE

Take a moment to think about your body.

Your mouth is needed to consume and chew food. Your brain is needed to think. Your legs and feet are needed to walk. And so on and so forth.

Now, your mouth absolutely loves to help you eat. Your brain's deepest desire is to help you think clearly. And your legs and feet are obsessed with helping you move around. God created each part of your body to love doing something different so that in fulfilling these desires, your body would be able to function fully.

Similarly, you are each a part of the Body of Christ, and as parts of a whole, each of you has been given different desires that God longs for you to live into in order to make the Body function properly. Fulfilling your role in the Body of Christ does not mean *giving up* what you love. It means *doing* what you love—that is, what God created you to do.

The *YOUCAT* tells us that God gave us "passions" or emotions so that "we might be attracted to what is right and good and repelled from what is evil and bad. . . . God made man in such a way that he can love and hate, desire or despise something, be attracted by some things and afraid of others, be full of joy, sorrow, or anger."[15] God created you with desire. He created you with things that you love and things that you hate. So He would not have created you to love something only to force you to do what you hate.

Saint Teresa of Calcutta had a deep desire to care for the poorest of the poor on the streets of India. The original religious order she was a part of did not allow her to even leave her home to help these people; instead, they asked her to teach the wealthy girls of that region of India. But God didn't leave her there. He had been the one to place the deep desire to care for the poor within her heart. So God called her to leave her

---

[15] Cardinal Christoph Schonborn, *Youcat: Youth Catechism of the Catholic Church* (San Francisco: Ignatius Press, 2011), 169–70.

order and start a new one. He did not force her to do something she hated in order to follow Him. Jesus knew the deepest passion in Saint Teresa's heart, and He called her to follow it.

Saint Thérèse of Lisieux wanted to join the convent at a young age. She was only fourteen years old when she asked to enter the Carmelite order of nuns, and she was fifteen when she was officially allowed to enter. God knew how difficult it would be for Thérèse to get permission to join the convent at such a young age, and yet He placed that desire within her heart for a reason. And because this is what she longed for, God did not force her to stay home. He allowed Thérèse to do what she loved, and so she became a nun at fifteen.

Your teacher is a teacher because she loves to teach. Perhaps one day, she woke up and said, "I want to be a teacher. I love youth and I love to teach." God did not hear this desire and say, "OK, but to follow me you have to be a doctor." He not only heard this desire, but He already knew it because He was the one who placed it on her heart. He knew that if your teacher were able to do what she loved, she would serve God better than if she did something she hated.

People get married because they love each other. They usually meet, date, decide they are in love, and eventually get engaged and married. God calls them to marry each other because He knows the deepest desires of their hearts. He knows that these two people will follow Him better together than they ever could apart. So He allows them to respond to the love they feel in their hearts.

We often think that to follow Jesus means giving up everything we love, because we see examples of saints who do just that. But the reality of it is that Saint Francis of Assisi did not give up all of his worldly possessions because God forced him to. Saint Francis became poor because that was how he desired to follow Christ. And so, while the way some saints choose to follow God may seem a little crazy to us, they are actually following a desire in their hearts.

The truth is, God knows the deepest desires of our hearts. He gives us those desires for a reason. He allows us to love certain things for a specific purpose. And He wants us to be able to do what we love.

Scripture affirms this in Psalm 37:4: "Delight yourself in the Lord; And He will give you the desires of your heart."

God wants us to love Him first above all else, and He wants to give us what we desire most. He knows what we love more intimately than anyone else, and when we find satisfaction in Him, He allows us to pursue what we love.

The goal is to first, follow Jesus; then, do what you desire. Saint Augustine of Hippo states this simply: "Love and do what you will."

Ask God to align your desires with His. Pray to Him, "God, change my heart. Help me to love what you love. Help me to love what you created me to love."

As we learned in our previous conversation, to follow Jesus—to love Him more than anything else—is to know that we are loved unconditionally by Him. The result of this is that God will allow us to do what we love to do. Because, as Saint Augustine believes, if we love God first, whatever we do will glorify Him.

God has created you with unique desires, and He plans to use these desires to set the world on fire. Because of this, following Christ will look different for everyone. But that's why you live within the Body of Christ—each of your individual desires is needed to allow the love of God to shine forth here on earth.

So, love God first, and pay attention to the desires that He has placed on your heart.

The saints are saints because they used their desires to glorify God. How can you do the same?

Discussion Questions:

What do you think it means to "delight yourself in the Lord"?

What are the current desires of your heart?

How do you think God might want you to use these desires to be the person He is creating you to be?

Quiet your heart. . . .

Ask your daughter for something specific that is on her heart—a dream, a worry, a troubled relationship—and pray for that desire or need.

Dear God,
Thank You for creating [your daughter's name] in such a unique way. Her likes and dislikes, her abilities, and her dreams make her so special. Help her to put You first in her life. Give her insight into what it means to love You and pursue You. May she turn to You in prayer every day, asking You to purify her heart. May she offer You her dreams and desires, and trust You to guide her. May she live out Proverbs 3:5: "Trust in the Lord with all your heart, and lean not on your own understanding. In all your ways, acknowledge him, and he will direct your paths."
Amen.

JOURNALING CONVERSATIONS

MOTHER: If you could go back to school, what would you like to study?

DAUGHTER: What is a class you'd love to take that isn't offered at school?

NOTES

Day 28

MEANT FOR GREATNESS

The world tells you to seek happiness. Jesus tells you to seek Him.

The world tells you to do whatever brings you the most pleasure. Jesus sometimes tells you to die to yourself.

The world tells you that being a Christian means you're always happy. Jesus tells you, "When you come to serve the Lord, prepare yourself for trials" (Sirach 2:1).

If this isn't uncomfortable, I don't know what is.

God is all-loving and kind, right? He created flowers and rainbows, right? Then why doesn't following Him mean constant happiness?

Many people think it does, and then when they encounter trials and difficulties they assume those difficulties are the result of bad behavior. People tend to run from discomfort; as a result, when they are unprepared to experience inevitable unhappiness, they run from Jesus when it comes.

But remember what Pope Benedict XVI said: "The world promises you comfort, but you were not made for comfort. You were made for greatness."

The world tells you lie after lie about what will make you happy.

Get the perfect boyfriend and you will be happy.
Wear the cutest clothes and you will be happy.
Go on the best vacations and you will be happy.
Get an A on every test and you will be happy.
Be popular and you will be happy.

The world tells you to run from the things that do not lead to this supposed happiness. But God wants more than happiness for you. He has *greatness* in store for you.

Let's talk about mountains. They are absolutely magnificent. They stretch high up in the sky; from the top of them it seems like you can see the entire world below. But getting to the top of a mountain can be a challenging experience. First of all, you do not begin at the top; you have to go on a journey to get there. You begin in the valley.

People often give the valley a lot of flak. When you stand in the valley, you are constantly looking up. Valleys are characteristically unhappy places. *National Geographic* describes valleys as follows:

> Valleys are depressed areas of land—scoured and washed out by the conspiring forces of gravity, water, and ice. Some hang; others are hollow. They all take the form of a "U" or "V."[16]

Mountains are described very differently:

> They define landscapes, people risk their lives to climb them, and they can even make their own weather.[17]

In other words, valleys are weak and mountains are powerful. Valleys are sad; mountains are happy. Valleys are negative; mountains are positive.

But nothing grows on the mountaintop.

Being a Christian does not mean you're always happy, because life would be meaningless without some pain and struggle. And constant comfort would not lead to greatness.

Now, don't get me wrong; everyone loves mountaintop experiences. They are great and fun and wonderful and beautiful. But sometimes God needs us to spend some time in the valley so that He can allow beautiful things to grow.

The thing about being a Christian is that we do not have a permanent residence in either location. We cannot spend all of our time on the mountain, just as we are not called to constantly be in the valley. God wants us to experience the goodness of the mountaintop *and* He wants us to experience growth in the valley.

---

16 *National Geographic*, "Valleys," National Geographic Partners, http://www.nationalgeographic.com/science/earth/surface-of-the-earth/valleys/.

17 *National Geographic*, "Mountains," National Geographic Partners, http://www.nationalgeographic.com/science/earth/surface-of-the-earth/mountains/.

As you know by now, Saint Teresa of Calcutta lived her entire life in pursuit of Christ. She was a Christian in the truest sense of the word—by all intents and purposes, she should have been happy.

But Mother Teresa tells us in one of her letters, "In my soul I feel just that terrible pain of loss—of God not wanting me—of God not being God—of God not really existing."[18] She spent a lot of time in the valley, *and* she was one of the greatest saints of our time.

If she experienced unhappiness in her life, you most certainly will, too. And I am convinced that Mother Teresa is a saint because of the time she spent in the valley.

Being a Christian does not mean that you will always be happy. Yes, God can satisfy your heart like nothing else in this world can, but that does not mean that He will always allow you to feel that satisfaction. Feelings are fleeting, but you are called to choose to love God even when you don't feel like it.

Prepare yourself for trials. Be ready for struggles. Know that your time in the valley will come. But when it does, guard your mind with the love of God. Remember the goodness of Christ that you have seen in your life. Bring the beauty of the mountaintop with you.

God does not desire unhappiness for you. He desires greatness for you. And sometimes that greatness will only come out of feelings that this world tells you to run from. But I encourage you not to run. Love Jesus even when you don't feel like it. When you do, you will experience the greatness that God has in store for you.

Discussion Questions:

Can you describe a mountaintop experience in your life?

Has there been a time in your life when you have been in the valley?

Can you see anything that grew—anything you learned—during your time in the valley?

---

[18] Kerry Walters, "Mother Teresa: A Saint Who Conquered Darkness," Franciscan Media, July 15, 2016, http://blog.franciscanmedia.org/mother-teresa-a-saint-who-conquered-darkness.

Quiet your heart. . . .

Ask your daughter for something specific that is on her heart—a dream, a worry, a troubled relationship—and pray for that desire or need.

Dear God,
Help [your daughter's name] to know that her feelings are never right or wrong. They are just feelings. Give her the courage to express them instead of stuffing them. But help both of us to manage our expectations about how we will feel throughout life. You never promise that we'll feel happy every minute of every day. Help us to expect trials and to prepare for them. When the times in the valley come, may we be shaped by them in good ways. Instead of giving up, growing bitter, or blaming You, may we look for the growth that always comes through difficult times, if we cooperate. And may we never forget that no matter how deep the valley, You are there with us and never let go of our hands.
Amen.

JOURNALING CONVERSATIONS

How do you act when you are overwhelmed? How do you feel about how many activities you're involved in?

MOTHER

DAUGHTER

NOTES

Day 29

GLORIFY GOD WITH YOUR BODY

We've all heard the saying, "Don't judge a book by its cover." Its what's on the inside that counts. This is good advice and a very true statement, but I can honestly say (and I'm sure you can relate) that nearly every book I have ever picked out to read has been chosen because it has a pretty cover.

We, as humans, are attracted to beauty. Mark Coker, the founder of indie book distributor Smashwords, explained this in a *Huffington Post* article, saying, "Our brains are wired to process images faster than words. When we see an image, it makes us feel something."[19]

Whether we are supposed to or not, we judge a book by its cover. Our brains are wired in a way that causes us to do so. Similarly, I would imagine that our brains process people's appearances faster than they do people's words or actions.

We judge people by their covers—their bodies.

Why?

Because a book's cover is just as much a part of the book as the text that's inside. Similarly, your body is just as much a part of you as what's in your soul. Your body and your soul are connected; they are not two separate things. And so, you must pay just as much attention to what your body has to say about your relationship with Christ as you do to what your soul has to say.

You know from experience that people judge you by your outward appearance. But it's possible that you have a skewed idea of *how* they judge you. And it's also possible that you care about how the wrong people see you.

---

[19] Terri Giuliano, "Yes, We Really Do Judge Books by Their Covers," *Huffpost*, May 30, 2013, http://www.huffingtonpost.com/2013/05/30/book-cover-design-indies_n_3354504.html.

The world tells you that you are more beautiful if you show off more of your skin. You might be convinced that makeup, tight-fitting clothes, crop tops, short shorts, and skimpy skirts will attract people to you. Many middle-schoolers (and older girls as well) define beauty according to the Kim Kardashians of the world and forget God's definition of beauty.

You tell yourself: "People know that I love God, so what does it matter if I want to fit in and wear crop tops and spandex? I go to church and wear a nice dress every Sunday, so why can't I wear a small bikini on Saturday? Everyone knows that I'm a good girl. They won't think any differently of me."

Many girls are busy convincing themselves that how they present themselves doesn't matter. But this is a lie.

Let's look at 1 Corinthians 6:12, 18–20. In this passage, Saint Paul is talking about the choices we make with our bodies:

> "Everything is lawful for me," but not everything is beneficial. "Everything is lawful for me," but I will not let myself be dominated by anything. . . . Avoid immorality. Every other sin a person commits is outside the body, but the immoral person sins against his own body. Do you not know that your body is a temple of the Holy Spirit within you, whom you have from God, and that you are not your own? For you have been purchased at a price. Therefore, glorify God in your body.

Let me tell you the truth: Despite the intentions in your heart, people will judge you based on your outward appearance. This may be unfair. I agree. We are not called to judge, and yet people do. And as Christians we are held to a higher standard in this regard because of the truth contained in Saint Paul's words.

How you present yourself does matter. Saint Paul tells you, "your body is a temple." Think about that for a moment. A temple is sacred. It is holy. It is set apart. It is unlike any other building in the world. People respect temples. They encounter God in temples.

If your body is a temple, then your body is sacred. It is holy. It is set apart. It is unlike anything else in this world. People should respect your body. They should encounter God in your body.

If your body is so special, don't you think it should be covered? Don't you think it should be protected?

I'm not saying you should wear turtlenecks in July (or at all). I'm not saying yoga pants are hands down the worst clothing item ever created. And I'm not saying every bathing suit should be burned.

But what I am saying is that you should protect what is holy.

When you get dressed in the morning, what is your intention? Is it to bring attention to your body or to bring attention to God?

You are beautiful, which means that some people will be attracted to your body for the wrong reasons, even if you wear a paper bag. But don't provoke that kind of attention. You can use your beauty to lead people to God or to lead them away from Him—which will you choose?

Emma Watson reminds girls, "The less you reveal the more people can wonder."

People should be in awe of the beautiful piece of God's creation that you are. People should look at you in wonder, recognizing you are an extraordinary temple. Dressing modestly does not make you any less beautiful. If anything, it reveals your beauty.

When people judge you by your cover, what will they assume is inside? I hope they see God.

Discussion Questions:

Are there certain fashions that you like but wonder if wearing them is glorifying God with your body?

When you get dressed in the morning, are you choosing clothes that highlight your body in a certain way in order to get attention?

Do you think that you are more likely to be respected by others if you show respect for your body with what you wear?

Quiet your heart. . . .

Ask your daughter for something specific that is on her heart—a dream, a worry, a troubled relationship—and pray for that desire or need.

Dear God,
Help [your daughter's name] to see how beautiful she is, and that leaving a little mystery by dressing in a modest way is beautiful. May she look at her body through Your eyes, recognizing that her body is a temple of the Holy Spirit. Wherever she goes, may she be protected and respected. May that respect start within her with the way that she sees and carries herself. May others see Jesus in [your daughter's name], instead of seeing her as a collection of body parts. May she know that she was purchased at a price, and that she is so valuable to You that You gave Your own Son in order to call her Your beloved daughter.
Amen.

JOURNALING CONVERSATIONS

What experience in your life would you like to erase?

MOTHER

DAUGHTER

NOTES

Day 30

FINDING YOUR SOUL MATE

Earlier, we learned that the idea that Christians are always happy is a lie. Happiness is fleeting and sometimes life is hard. Today we will talk about a related lie: When the right boy comes along, I will be happy.

Here is the truth: If you expect a human (much less a boy) to make you happy, you will consistently be disappointed.

Taylor Swift has been a role model for girls for the past decade, and during that time she has brought her fans through romance after romance, breakup after breakup. Every time she dates someone new she thinks she has found "the one." Her song lyrics are upbeat and hopeful. Clearly she's happy when she sings lines like:

This night is sparkling, don't you let it go. I'm wonderstruck, blushing all the way home.

I don't wanna dance if I'm not dancing with you.

You belong with me.

And then a few months later, her songs take a turn for the worse. She goes through another breakup because she's no longer happy, and we have to sing along to lyrics like:

He's the reason for the teardrops on my guitar.

We are never, ever, ever getting back together.

As far as I'm concerned you're just another picture to burn.

Taylor Swift seems to think that when she finds the right boy, or her "soul mate," so to speak, she will be happy. And then he doesn't make her happy. And then they break up. Because apparently that means he's not "the one." He's not her "soul mate."

The world tells you that when the right boy comes along, you will be happy. But this is a lie. The truth is, there is only *one* man who can satisfy the desires of your heart.

When you were much younger, you might have heard the story of *The Runaway Bunny* by Margaret Wise Brown. In this book, the bunny wants to run away. The minute that statement is out of his mouth, his mother assures him that she will run after him, each and every time, because he belongs to her. The little bunny tries to come up with as many far-off places to run to as he can imagine. He says he'll become a fish in a trout stream, or a rock on a high mountain, or a sailboat heading far away. Regardless of what he thinks he could become, the mother bunny explains that nothing would prevent her from following him. She would never give up; she would never turn back; she would always pursue him. "Shucks," says the little bunny finally, "I might just as well stay where I am and be your little bunny." So he does, and the mother gives him a carrot.

It doesn't matter where the bunny would go; his mother would follow. In that same way, Jesus never stops pursuing you. The little bunny constantly runs away from the person who loves him the most, and each time he does, he changes his identity. He thinks each identity will bring him happiness, but by the end of the story he learns that he only has true happiness with his mother. She gives him the carrot, which he has desired.

When you date people with the assumption that this particular person will make you happy, you can end up running from the only man who can truly satisfy your heart. In turning toward a boyfriend and seeking fulfillment, you can inadvertently turn away from Jesus, your true soul mate—the one who holds the "carrot" you desire most.

Scripture describes God with these words: "You open your hand and satisfy the desire of every living thing" (Psalm 145:16). Jesus is the only one who can satisfy your desires. His hand is constantly open and outstretched toward you; all you need to do is reach out and take hold of it. Only then will you be truly fulfilled.

I want to encourage you to stop looking for a boy to satisfy your heart—to stop looking for a boy to make you happy. Look to God and God alone. Allow Him to satisfy your heart first. Quit running. Choose Him first, because He has already chosen you. And when the time is right, God will allow just the right boy to pursue you. Just remember the words of pastor and author Max Lucado: "A girl's heart should be so lost in God that a man must go through Him in order to find her."

Discussion Questions:

What are some words you would use to describe the way Jesus feels about you?

What are some ways you can tell if someone is interested in you for the right reasons and truly has your interests at heart?

What is a way you can have your longings satisfied by God?

Quiet your heart. . . .

Ask your daughter for something specific that is on her heart—a dream, a worry, a troubled relationship—and pray for that desire or need.

Dear God,
Thank You for loving us so much that You pursue us. You call us beautiful, You see the depths of who we are, and You always come to rescue us. There is no Prince Charming like You—the Prince of Peace. May we go to You to have our longings fulfilled. May we turn to You when we need affirmation. May we fix our eyes on You when we feel lonely. Help us to remember the truth that if we expect a person to fill up what is empty inside us, we will always be disappointed. May we go to You first.
Amen.

JOURNALING CONVERSATIONS

MOTHER: My first crush and what I learned from the experience:

DAUGHTER: What I wish I knew about boys:

Day 31

SAY NO TO DRAMA

In what ways have you experienced drama at school?
[Let your daughter answer.]

There are all sorts of examples of drama that can be experienced at your age. A lot of people would say you can't help being caught up in it. Kids might talk behind your back, message behind your back, insult you to your face, give you the silent treatment, exclude you from the group, or invite you and then ignore you. The possibilities seem endless; kids can be both creative and cruel.

Are we stuck? Is there nothing we can do to avoid it? You may think that you can't avoid drama. But the truth is that being caught up in drama is a choice, and you can choose to avoid it.

Are you surprised that I'm saying being caught up in drama is a choice? Are you thinking, "But even if I choose not to do the things that cause drama, they might still happen. So how can it be a choice to be caught up in drama?"

The key phrase to pay attention to is "being caught up." When we're caught up in something, it's all we're thinking about. We are allowing it to be the source of our joy or to steal our joy, and we're often making it the most important thing. We can't help it if something happens, but we can choose whether we'll be caught up in it and allow it to take a place in our hearts reserved for the things that matter most. You have more power over drama than you might think.

Galatians 1:10 talks about this: "Am I now seeking the favor of men, or of God? Or am I trying to please men? If I were still pleasing men, I should not be a servant of Christ."

This verse says you need to decide whose approval you are after. You can decide to go after people's approval and make that the most important thing. You can make pleasing people so important that if someone is unhappy with you, you'll feel awful; you'll feel terrible about yourself; you'll feel worthless. You can decide that you are going to measure how good your day was by how the girls at school have treated you. And this is the way most girls live. If this verse were posed to them as a question—"Are you seeking human approval, or God's approval?"—if they were honest, they'd say they were after people's approval.

But just because most girls live like that doesn't mean it's the best way to live. In fact, if you choose to live that way, you'll always be insecure. Your emotions will yo-yo every day. You'll never really be able to count on feeling good, because you never know what someone might do or say.

So what's the alternative? How can you choose to avoid drama?

You can decide that no one's approval matters more than God's. You can choose to trust that when He made you, He knew what He was doing. You can choose to believe that He made you just the way He wanted you, and He thinks you are His masterpiece. You can choose to stop comparing yourself to other girls. In the words of Saint Thérèse of Lisieux, "If every tiny flower wanted to be a rose, spring would lose its loveliness." You'll come to see that God is creative, and He likes variety. He doesn't want you to be just like everyone else. He made you uniquely you, and He did this on purpose.

When you find yourself facing drama, you have a choice to lean into it or to run in the other direction. You can keep an eye out for drama and avoid it. If your instinct is to fight back with nasty words, you can choose to close your mouth and walk away. If your instinct is to shut down and try to bury your emotions, you can choose to confide in someone who is wise and calm, or to journal what you are feeling. If your instinct is to talk negatively to yourself or rehash the unkind things someone has said about you, you can choose to remember the truths about how God sees you.

In each and every action, you can ask yourself, "Whose approval am I trying to win right now?" If the answer is anyone other than God, then you are on shaky ground, which leads to feeling insecure. But if you choose to live for His approval more than anyone else's, you will end every day remembering that you are surrounded and covered by God's unconditional, never-ending, unfailing love and acceptance.

Discussion Questions:

What kinds of social drama have you experienced or witnessed?

Can you think of ways that you can avoid drama at school?

In what ways can you focus on God's approval rather than other people's approval?

Quiet your heart. . . .

Ask your daughter for something specific that is on her heart—a dream, a worry, a troubled relationship—and pray for that desire or need.

Dear God,
Help [your daughter's name] to desire Your approval more than anyone else's. Help her to see that she has the power to make choices, freeing her from situations in which she feels stuck. She can choose to walk away from drama, and to walk toward You and Your perspective on the situation. She can ask You, "God, have I done anything wrong?" And if the answer is no, then she can choose to rest in the fact that You made her just as she is, You love her, and it is enough. If the answer is yes, she can immediately ask your forgiveness and commit to apologizing to anyone she has hurt. Help her to fill her mind with what You think of her instead of focusing on what other people think. May Your approval matter more than anyone else's.
Amen.

JOURNALING CONVERSATIONS

What are your favorite and least favorite things to do as a family?

MOTHER

DAUGHTER

Day 32

SOUL FRIENDS

How do I know the difference between a toxic friendship and a good one?
[Let your daughter answer.]

How do I know if my friends are true friends?
[Let your daughter answer.]

Let's talk about this more by looking at some stereotypical ways girls treat each other. These are stereotypes, so there will obviously always be exceptions to the rule. But I think that as you listen to what I'm describing, you'll know what I'm talking about.

I don't need to tell you that there are a lot of dynamics at play among girls. Cliques, groups of friends, are complicated and multilayered, and very often girls play certain roles within them. The role you play can change depending on the group of girls you are with. And your role within a group can change. You can also be a combination of a couple of roles.

In her book *Queen Bees and Wannabes*, author Rosalind Wiseman describes these roles as the queen bee and her court.[20] I know that none of us like to be labeled. You might not appreciate these names. But do your best to look past the labels in order to get smarter about the way you are interacting with other girls. Not everything I share will ring true for you, and that's OK. I'm just giving you some insights into what goes on among most girls. I'm really hoping that some of what you hear will help you to see that when things come up in friendship that are really hard, it's not always about you. It's not always something you've done. There are dynamics in play, roles in place, that can create drama and heartache even when you aren't doing anything wrong. But there are things you probably are doing that are keeping this unhealthy way of relating to each other going, so knowledge can be power if it helps you start to make better choices.

---

[20] Rosalind Wiseman, *Queen Bees and Wannabes: Helping Your Daughter Survive Cliques, Gossip, Boys, and the New Realities of Girl World*, 3rd ed. (New York: Harmony Books, 2016), 29.

Queen Bee

What are some ways you'd describe a Queen Bee?
[Let your daughter answer.]

Wiseman describes her in this way: "Through a combination of charisma, force, money, looks, will and social intelligence, this girl reigns supreme over other girls and weakens their friendships with others, which strengthens her own power and influence…You're on her side, or else. You're either with her or against her."[21]

Sidekick

The Sidekick is the second in command, the Queen Bee's closest friend. She backs up the Queen Bee no matter what because her own power comes from her relationship with the Queen. Together, they seem to other girls like an impenetrable force.[22]

Banker

Wiseman writes, "Information about others is currency in Girl World—whoever has the most information has the most power."[23] The Banker is the collector of this currency, and she uses it to gain power and create chaos. She collects information about other girls and waits to share it until just the right moment—when it serves her well.

Messenger

There are similarities between the roles of the Messenger and the Banker. Both gather and trade information about other girls. But the Messenger shares the information (the gossip) in order to be perceived as useful by the other girls. She loves to step in to help reconcile disagreements—but while she appears to be saving the day and just wanting everyone to get along, she is actually creating drama and thrives on it.[24]

Pleaser/Wannabe

The Pleaser/Wannabe will do whatever it takes to stay in favor with the Queen Bee or the Sidekick. She tends to copy others' behavior, clothing, and interests but never feels a sense of belonging.[25] She's on the edge of the group and she knows it. The Pleaser lacks personal boundaries and will do things she knows are wrong just to avoid being excluded or to get the chance to gain the approval of the Queen Bee.

Torn Bystander

The Torn Bystander can see what is wrong in the social group, and her conscience is bothered by the poor treatment of other girls. That being said, she doesn't want to

---

[21] Ibid., 29.
[22] Ibid., 34.
[23] Ibid., 35.
[24] Ibid., 36.
[25] Ibid., 37.

stand up for anyone being bullied, out of fear that she might be next. She convinces herself that the little she could do wouldn't make much of a difference anyway.[26]

Target

Most people can easily pick out the target. She's the one who is being made fun of, excluded, and teased. You might assume she isn't part of the group, but that isn't necessarily the case. No one wants to be the Target, but this girl does have one clear advantage. She sees these "friendship games" for what they are, and the day she tastes real friendship, she knows she has discovered a treasure worth keeping. If the Target is smart, she'll step out of this situation and pursue true friendship elsewhere.

Champion

What's unique about the Champion? Wiseman writes, "she can take criticism, doesn't make people choose friends, and doesn't blow off someone for a better offer. She has friends in different groups and doesn't treat people differently when groups are together. She can and will stand up to the Queen Bee in a way that treats them both with dignity."[27]

What might change in your friend group if you all decided to have more Champion moments? If you were willing to recognize bad behavior and call it out? If you were willing to be true to yourselves, even if it meant being willing to stand alone at times? What might change in terms of your own level of happiness if you looked at the people you are choosing to spend the most time with, those you are investing in as friends? As it says in Proverbs 18:24, "There are friends who bring ruin, but there are true friends more loyal than a brother."

Saint Francis de Sales puts it this way: "Love everyone with a deep love based on charity. . . but form friendship only with those who can share virtuous things with you."

You are called to love everyone, but you are called to enter into a deep relationship only with those who will help you to grow in virtue. In other words, you are called to enter into a deep friendship only with those who will help you to grow into the person God is calling you to be.

Let's call these God-given friends "soul friends." Soul friends are different. They are set apart from all the other people in your life. A soul friend is someone who leads you to God. This type of friend tends to your soul and cares for you on a spiritual level. She asks you the hard questions like "How's your heart?" or "How is your relationship with

---

[26] Ibid., 39.
[27] Ibid., 42.

God?" or "What are you struggling with right now?" If you desire to follow God, you must keep these types of friends close to you.

If you are striving to be a saint, you must surround yourself with people who point you to heaven. Soul friends will lovingly and gently help you reach heaven. They will challenge you. They will lead you to the sacraments. They will bless you. They will listen to your brokenness and they will call you beloved. They will want what's best for you, and they will help you to discover God's will for your life.

I challenge you to be open to the soul friends that God places in your life. These friends won't necessarily be ones you naturally gravitate toward. What pulls you together isn't your common interest in a hobby or a sport you play together. These intentional relationships are built and nurtured because of the common focus on Christ and the desire to help each other grow spiritually.

Think about your group of friends. Think about the girls you surround yourself with. Do any of them care for your heart? Do any of them challenge you in your prayer life? Do any of them lead you closer to Christ?

If you think of a friend or a group of friends who do this for you, I encourage you to pour into them. Be vulnerable with them and allow them to see the deepest parts of your heart. I am aware that this can be terrifying, but I am also aware that this can lead to a friendship that you will treasure. But something important to remember is that these sorts of friendships don't just happen. They are formed when you decide to put in the time to get to know someone in a deeper way. It might require moving out of your comfort zone and proactively talking about things that don't seem natural to bring up. I challenge you to persevere through any awkwardness in order to experience a treasured friendship on the other side.

Discussion Questions:

Who are your closest friends?

Do any of them care for your heart? Do any of them challenge you in your prayer life? Do any of them lead you closer to Christ?

If not, who is a girl you may not know well right now but you sense might be open to a deeper, spiritually focused friendship?

Quiet your heart. . . .

Ask your daughter for something specific that is on her heart—a dream, a worry, a troubled relationship—and pray for that desire or need.

Dear God,
I pray that You would provide [your daughter's name] with deep soul friends. Surround her with a few girls who care about her heart, are trustworthy, encourage her and tell her what is wonderful about her, and lead her closer to You. I pray that [your daughter's name] would be that kind of friend to others. Instead of settling for superficial fun (although there's nothing wrong with that) I pray she would put in the work and the time required to have a true soul friend. Bind their hearts together, Lord, with cords that cannot be broken. Be at their center and draw them closer to You.
Amen.

JOURNALING CONVERSATIONS

What are things you find hard in friendship?

MOTHER

DAUGHTER

Day 33

TOXIC FRIENDSHIPS

Last time we discussed the beauty of soul friends. Maybe you have some in your life right now and maybe you don't, but either way, I pray that at some point in your life, you will be surrounded by a community of friends where you are learning how to love and care for those people well.

Today we're going to continue talking about what to look for and what to avoid in a friend. Let's start with what we should avoid. Here are some qualities that are found in toxic friendships:

- Using information to gain power or manipulate
- Telling people who they can be friends with
- Jealousy
- Sarcasm
- Gossip
- Blowing people off
- Being self-serving or self-centered
- Rewriting history when confronted
- Lack of honesty

Do you have any friendships with these qualities?
[Let your daughter answer.]

What draws you back to a friendship in which you are treated poorly?
[Let your daughter answer.]

These are qualities found in healthy friendships:

- All have separate interests.
- They allow each other to have other friends.

- They are happy for each other instead of jealous.
- They support each other when things are hard instead of withdrawing.
- They joke with each other but know what each feels sensitive about.
- They tell each other how they feel.
- If they are angry, they address it—they don't sit on it.

But even if your friendship is healthy, that doesn't mean it's going to be perfect. There will be times when you both need to apologize. What's the best way to do that?

- Know and acknowledge what you did. Don't try to put the best spin on your actions or justify your behavior.
- Only talk about what you did—this is not the time to include what the other person did.
- Don't bury an insult in the apology. ("I'm sorry you're so sensitive that you need an apology, but here—I'm sorry.")
- Give the apology without justifying your actions.
- Don't expect an apology in return. If it comes, great, but don't expect it.
- Use the words "Do you forgive me?" It's far more impactful than simply saying, "I'm sorry."

If someone apologizes to you, don't respond by saying, "It's OK." That negates the importance of your feelings. Instead say, "Thank you for apologizing. That really means a lot to me."

Jesus has taught us to forgive always, but that doesn't mean we don't recognize bad patterns of friendship and either step out of the friendship or insist that things change. There are things that poison friendship, and unless you get rid of them, the friendship will remain toxic, regardless of how many times people say they are sorry.

One poison to friendship is sarcasm. Typically we use sarcasm in a joking manner, but more often than not, it can be cutting and hurtful to whomever it is being spoken to.

In true friendship, we are called to build each other up, not tear each other down. Our words must be used to bring peace, love, and joy to one another. You may think your sarcastic words are completely harmless, but are they building up your friends? Are they bringing joy to your friends? Are they causing your friends to feel loved? In healthy friendships, words matter and are chosen carefully.

Another poison to friendship is gossip. Let me just say that for girls, this one can be especially difficult. Gossip can be sneaky because if we are not careful, it can take on the appearance of any other innocent conversation. But gossip is one of the most hurtful things to a friendship.

In the book of Sirach we are warned against people who gossip: "Cursed be gossips and the double-tongued, for they destroy the peace of many" (Sirach 28:13). Gossip destroys peace. And it's more than just saying bad things behind someone's back. Gossip is revealing any secret information—good or bad—about another person without their knowledge or permission. Healthy friendships must be built on a foundation of trust, and gossip destroys trust.

Gossip can be very easy to fall into, which means you must be very intentional to avoid it. In friendships, I encourage you never to be the person to start gossip. Never talk about someone behind their back. I challenge you to walk away from gossip. If you enter into a group of girls talking about another girl, walk away. And if it happens to be your soul friends who are gossiping, ask them to stop. Call them higher. If it is your job to lead your friends to Christ, it is also your job to lead them away from gossip.

The last poison I want to mention is jealousy. In a true Christ-centered relationship, you should strive to complement each other, not compete with each other. God gifts each and every one of us differently, and those gifts are beautiful and unique for a reason. He needs every person to have different gifts because everyone is called to live their life for Christ differently. So don't envy your friend's gifts. Instead, affirm those gifts.

I challenge you to pay attention to how sarcasm, gossip, and jealousy pop up in your friendships. Specifically, I challenge you to pull one friend aside today or tomorrow and ask them to help you to avoid these poisons in your life. That's what it means to hold each other accountable.

That being said, I also challenge you to love your friends where they are. Some people will struggle with these poisons more than others, and it is important that you not condemn your friends, that you instead respond to their struggles with love and encouragement.

As Saint Teresa of Calcutta says to us, "Don't expect your friend to be a perfect person. But, help your friend to become a perfect person. That's true friendship." Help your friends become more perfect people. Help them strive to be saints by kicking these friendship poisons to the curb.

Discussion Questions:

Which of the poisons to friendship is the most tempting to you: sarcasm, gossip, or jealousy?

Which of your friends could you ask to hold you accountable in one of these areas of struggle?

If you encountered some girls gossiping, what is something you could say to try to move the conversation in a new direction?

Quiet your heart. . . .

Ask your daughter for something specific that is on her heart—a dream, a worry, a troubled relationship—and pray for that desire or need.

Dear God,
I know that if I want the kind of friendship we've talked about—one that is free from sarcasm, gossip, and jealousy—I need to start with myself. Please forgive me for making sarcastic comments. Please forgive me for gossiping. Please forgive me for being jealous. Please replace the sarcasm with encouragement, the gossip with words of affirmation, and the jealousy with a desire to see the other person receive what is best. Please help me to grow in humility, and in doing so, to become more like You in friendship.
Amen.

JOURNALING CONVERSATIONS

Do you feel emotionally safe in your friendships? Do you feel like you have to wear a mask to fit in?

MOTHER

DAUGHTER

NOTES

Day 34

YOU ARE WHAT YOU LOVE

Think about your favorite song.
Now think about your favorite TV show.
Now think about your favorite movie.

As you focus on these favorite things, think about how they affect you. Have you ever found yourself watching a love story and then realizing that you desire the same type of love? Have you ever listened to a song and suddenly decided that, just like the artist, you have a strong desire to do exactly what they are doing? We listen to certain music to put us in a particular mood for a reason.

You see, what we listen to and watch affects what we love.

When we listen to country music, we might find ourselves full of a desire to be sitting on the beach, basking in the sun, and sipping sweet tea. When we watch a Nicholas Sparks movie, we might suddenly desire a risky and intense love story of our own.

What we feed our minds and souls affects the desires of our minds and souls. According to theologian James K. A. Smith, "Our wants and longings and desires are at the core of our identity, the wellspring from which our actions and behavior flow."[28] Or as Saint Augustine said, "You are what you love."

And so, if what we love is affected by what we watch and listen to, and if what we love is the core of our identity, then we will become what we watch and listen to.

So what's our truth today? What we watch and listen to matters. Smith goes on to tell his readers that we must learn to be "attentive and intentional about what we love."[29]

---

[28] James K. A. Smith, *You Are What You Love: The Spiritual Power of Habit* (Grand Rapids, MI: Brazos Press, 2016), 2.
[29] Ibid.

This goes back to what we've talked about a lot: intentionality. Instead of just letting life happen to you, you have been challenged to stop and think about who you spend time with, how you act with them, how much you share, and where the friendship is taking you. I want to challenge you to apply that same intentionality to what goes into your mind, ears, and eyes. Is what you are listening to or watching a blessing to your life or a poison? Does what you are listening to and watching point you to God or to someone or something you are not called to love?

It's been said that falling in love determines everything you do. A priest by the name of Pedro Arrupe said, "What you are in love with, what seizes your imagination, will affect everything. It will decide what gets you out of bed in the mornings, what you do with your evenings, how you spend your weekends, what you read, who you know, what breaks your heart, and what amazes you with joy and gratitude. Fall in love, stay in love, and it will decide everything." What you are in love with will determine everything that you do. It will transform who you are. You are what you love.

Our world today tells us that if we truly know who we are, what we watch and listen to doesn't matter. But if we are operating under the assumption that this is false and that what we absorb does affect what we love, then we need to ask ourselves what we *want* to love. What will you allow to influence everything that you do? What will you allow to determine who you become?

Of course, we can't always control who or what we fall in love with, but we can control who or what we *choose* to love.

The one person we are called to choose to love for the entirety of our lives is Jesus. We should feed our minds and souls with Him. He is the love who should determine all that we do and all that we are. Jesus is the one who should seize our imagination, get us out of bed in the morning, decide what we do with our evenings and weekends, and determine what we read, who we know, what breaks our hearts, and what amazes us with joy and gratitude. If we fall in love with Jesus and stay in love with Him, it will point everything in our lives in the right direction.

And what's super cool about Jesus is that falling in love primarily with Him will affect every other love in your life. Smith explains it this way: "Jesus is a teacher who doesn't just inform our intellect but forms our very loves. . . . Jesus' command to follow Him is a command to align our loves and longings with his—to want what God wants, to desire what God desires . . ."[30]

---

[30] Ibid.

If we fill our minds and souls with Jesus, then everything else that we naturally desire will be in line with His will. But if we fill our minds and souls with a countless number of things in our world that are not of Jesus, then our natural desires will not be in line with what God wants for us.

And unfortunately, in our world, it is much easier to fall in love with the wrong things than to fall in love with Jesus. So I encourage you to memorize and regularly pray the following prayer:

Dear God,
Change my heart. Help me to love what You love. Help me to love what You created me to love. Amen.

Train yourself to daily ask God to teach you to fall in love with Him.

So my question to you today is this: Will you allow Jesus to shape what you love, or will you allow the world to shape what you love?

The world will try to make you fall in love with all that it has to offer. It will wrap up lies in beautifully composed song lyrics and seemingly harmlessly entertaining TV shows and movies. You will be tempted to become a part of the world because you will be tempted to fall in love with it rather than with the truth of Jesus Christ.

God has always known this would be a pitfall. That's why in the book of Proverbs He warned us: "With all vigilance guard your heart, for in it are the sources of life" (4:23).

Life starts in the heart, so we must guard our hearts. We must keep watch and guard against the lies of this world because we are what we love. Remember this truth today: You will begin to resemble whatever it is that you spend your time doing. You will become like whatever or whoever you choose to love.

I leave you with this challenge: This week, surround yourself with more things and people that point you toward Jesus. Replace at least one song a day with something that directs your gaze to God. Read something new this week that talks about Jesus. Choose to love Jesus and all of the things that lead you to Him. Allow Jesus to be the one you fall in love with, and then allow this love to transform who you are. Allow yourself to be like Jesus.

Discussion Questions:

What does your media diet consist of?

Where are some places you can find movies, songs, and shows that point you toward Christ?

Do you agree or disagree that you are what you love? Why?

Quiet your heart. . . .

Ask your daughter for something specific that is on her heart—a dream, a worry, a troubled relationship—and pray for that desire or need.

Dear God,
It's sometimes hard to know where to find entertainment that's clean. It seems like everywhere we turn, there is trash that is very appealing on the surface. Please give us the inner strength to keep searching until we find entertainment that is good for us. Help us to encounter true beauty and to feast on it. Instead of settling for junk food, may we long for art and media that truly feeds our souls. May we fall in love with You, first and foremost, and may our love for You and Yours for us change everything.
Amen.

JOURNALING CONVERSATIONS

If you could be a character in a film or a TV show, who would you be and why?

MOTHER

DAUGHTER

NOTES

Day 35

SOCIAL MEDIA

According to a 2017 survey of 2,000 girls and boys ages 12 to 24, 79 percent of people in this age group use Snapchat, 76 percent use Facebook, 73 percent use Instagram, and 40 percent use Twitter.[31] A 2014 study revealed that more than 50 percent of children have used an online social network by the time they are 10.[32]

That was a few years ago. Imagine what that percentage is today.

What's important about these statistics is that people begin to use social media (and a lot of it) at a very young age, and the majority will continue to do so throughout their lifetime.

Here's the thing about social media. It can be a wonderful way to gain access to your friends and family no matter where they are in the world. Social media connects people from all over and allows relationships to flourish in ways that they couldn't a couple of decades ago. But social media can also be extremely dangerous, because it provides a space to be whoever you want to be. Freeing? Yes. Dangerous? Absolutely.

I think you know that social media can be damaging. I think you know how tempting it can be to base your worth on how many likes or comments you get (we've talked about this before). But what you may not know is how dangerous a false sense of authenticity can be on social media platforms.

The key to a positive experience with social media is transparency. In fact, the key to most things is transparency. Are you truly who you say you are? Is your identity consistent, or do you wear a variety of masks?

---

[31] "Reach of Leading Social Media and Networking Sites Used by Teenagers and Young Adults in the United States as of February 2017," Statista, https://www.statista.com/statistics/199242/social-media-and-networking-sites-used-by-us-teenagers/.

[32] "More Than Half of Children Use Social Media by the Age of 10: Facebook Is Most Popular Site That Youngsters Join," *Daily Mail*, November 19, 2014, http://www.dailymail.co.uk/news/article-2552658/More-half-children-use-social-media-age-10-Facebook-popular-site-youngsters-join.html.

In the Gospels, we learn that Jesus cared so much about authenticity and transparency that He told people not to follow the example of those who have multiple identities. In Matthew 23:1–3, Jesus acknowledged that the scribes and the Pharisees had authority because of their hierarchical position, but He also warned people against following their example. Jesus saw that the Pharisees said one thing and did another. Because of that, He warned against trusting or following them.

This goes back to the old adages "Practice what you preach" and "You can't just talk the talk; you have to walk the walk." You cannot be one person in "real life" and another person on social media. Social media *is* real life. And just as people will judge you based on your outward appearance (modest or showing lots of skin), they will judge you based on how you present yourself on social media.

Think about your own social media posts. Do you only post things that reveal your authentic self? Do you ever post things that you wouldn't want certain people in your life to see? Do you have any fake social media accounts on which you post things that you wouldn't post anywhere else? Is what you say to other people on social media consistent with what you would say to them in person?

Our world tells you that what you post on social media doesn't matter. But this is a lie. The truth is that what you post on social media is an outward reflection of who you are. So be true to yourself when you are online.

I'm sure you're familiar with the acronym WWJD (What Would Jesus Do?). As cheesy and overused as it is, it is applicable to us on social media and at many other points in our lives. When you are posting on social media, think to yourself, "What would Jesus do?" Or even better, "What would Jesus think?"

What would Jesus do? Jesus probably wouldn't use social media. Actually, I take that back. Who knows, He would probably have a supercool social media account for evangelization purposes (things we'll never know, I guess).

But what would Jesus *think*? That's a huge question. Because here's the truth: Jesus follows you on every social media account you have or will ever have. He follows the real ones and the fake ones. And guess what. He also follows you in person. Jesus knows the truest you and the fakest you. So, knowing that Jesus is one of your followers, ask yourself: "Do I want Jesus to see this post? Would I want Him to see this comment or that tweet?"

I'm not telling you today to delete your social media accounts (well, maybe the fake ones). But I am challenging you to live an authentic life. Be true to who you are at all times and remember that who you are online is a reflection of you.

So today, I specifically challenge you to take a good, hard look at your social media accounts. Ask yourself if the person you are looking at online is the same person who is in your heart. Ask yourself if Jesus would be pleased with your social media profile. And if the answer to either of those questions is no, then go ahead and delete everything on your account that represents an inauthentic version of you. I promise you, the freedom that will come from living authentically will be worth any loss.

Discussion Questions:

What do you think about the spam accounts? Do you think they are harmful or harmless?

What is the hardest part of being authentic online?

Who do you know who makes good use of social media? Whose example you could follow?

Quiet your heart. . . .

Ask your daughter for something specific that is on her heart—a dream, a worry, a troubled relationship—and pray for that desire or need.

Dear God,
You are the creator of all good things and the source of all creativity. I pray You'd help us to use social media in a way that draws people closer together and encourages them. Help us to stop using it as a way we try to impress or compare ourselves to others. Help us to be the same people online that we are in our face-to-face interactions. Please help us to never consider electronic connection a substitute for in-person communication. May You be pleased with who we are online, in person, and when we are quietly by ourselves.
Amen.

JOURNALING CONVERSATIONS

What are your best and worst personality traits?

MOTHER

DAUGHTER

Day 36

DOUBTING THOMAS

Today we're going to give some time to the disciple Thomas, because you just might have a lot in common with him. Thomas was a follower of Jesus, and he spent his life traveling and telling everyone he could about his friend Jesus. But before he started doing this, he really doubted Him.

We read his story in John 20:19–29:

> On the evening of that first day of the week, when the doors were locked where the disciples were for fear of the Jews, Jesus came and stood in their midst and said to them, "Peace be with you." When he had said this, he showed them his hands and his side. The disciples rejoiced when they saw the Lord.
>
> [Jesus] said to them again, "Peace be with you. As the Father has sent me, so I send you. And when he had said this, he breathed on them and said to them, "Receive the holy Spirit. Whose sins you forgive are forgiven them, and whose sins you retain are retained."
>
> Thomas, called Didymus, one of the Twelve, was not with them when Jesus came. So the other disciples said to him, "We have seen the Lord."
>
> But he said to them, "Unless I see the mark of the nails in his hands and put my finger into the nail marks and put my hand into his side, I will not believe."
>
> Now a week later his disciples were again inside and Thomas was with them. Jesus came, although the doors were locked, and stood in their midst and said, "Peace be with you." Then he said to Thomas, "Put your finger here and see my hands, and bring your hand and put it into my side, and do not be unbelieving, but believe."
>
> Thomas answered and said to him, "My Lord and my God!"

> Jesus said to him, "Have you come to believe because you have seen me? Blessed are those who have not seen and have believed."

Even though Jesus was standing in front of Thomas, he needed even more proof to believe that Jesus really was who He claimed to be. Thomas wasn't satisfied with looking at Jesus; he needed to touch His wounds to believe that He really was the Son of God and had risen from the dead. And Thomas knew Jesus personally! He had journeyed with Him for years and he still doubted!

Because of this, our friend here is often called Doubting Thomas. Sometimes this name is viewed in a negative light, but I think if we are honest, we would have to admit that we all can be doubting Thomases at times.

And that's OK. It is OK to doubt.

Throughout our conversations we have talked about many of the lies that our world tells us, and we've encountered the truth in Jesus' words in Scripture. But today we are going to do something slightly different. Today, we are going to take a look at a lie that religious people might tell us. Sometimes people who go to church very faithfully tell us that to love God means we can't question or doubt. But this is a lie. The truth is that some of Jesus' closest friends questioned Him and we can, too.

Saint Augustine (one of the greatest saints of all time) said, "Doubt is another element of faith." He claimed that doubt and faith do not contradict each other. In fact, doubt is a part of faith. You cannot have faith without doubt. So, just because you doubt doesn't mean that you don't have faith.

"Doubting Thomas" is a saint, so there has to be hope for us, too!

It's very likely that Thomas had deep love for Jesus even as he doubted. His questioning might show just how much he loved and cared for and wanted to know about Jesus. Thomas' desire for closeness to Jesus likely drove his desire to know, with greater proof and assurance, that Jesus was truly alive.

I think that we all need to strive to be comfortable enough in our faith to doubt. Jesus welcomes our doubt because it forces us to lean into Him. Doubting means that we care. If we didn't care about Jesus, we wouldn't bother to ask questions. But asking questions is a sign that we are trying to understand, so ask all the questions that you want.

You are in the perfect place to ask questions. You are surrounded by adults who want to try to answer any questions that you may have about your faith, so don't be afraid to ask. Allow your doubt to transform your faith.

Discussion Questions:

Has anyone ever made you feel it is wrong to doubt?

Do you feel free to ask questions about your faith?

What are three questions you have about God, Jesus, or your faith?

Quiet your heart. . . .

Ask your daughter for something specific that is on her heart—a dream, a worry, a troubled relationship—and pray for that desire or need.

My Lord God, I have no idea where I am going. I do not see the road ahead of me. I cannot know for certain where it will end. Nor do I really know myself, and the fact that I think I am following your will does not mean that I am actually doing so. But I believe that the desire to please you does in fact please you. And I hope I have that desire in all that I am doing. I hope that I will never do anything apart from that desire. And I know that if I do this you will lead me by the right road, though I may know nothing about it. Therefore I will trust you always though I may seem to be lost and in the shadow of death. I will not fear, for you are ever with me, and you will never leave me to face my perils alone. —Thomas Merton

JOURNALING CONVERSATIONS

For mom: Who was your favorite teacher or coach when you were in middle school and why?

For daughter: Who is your favorite teacher or coach and why?

MOTHER

DAUGHTER

Day 37

CONFESSION

No doubt about it, our view of God will affect how we feel about the sacrament of confession. Some of us think of God as a stern father or an authoritarian dictator. We might picture Him with a face of constant disapproval. We think to ourselves, "Why go to confession and spend time in front of someone who is never going to approve of me, anyway? Why bother? I'll never be good enough."

Some of us think of God as an indulgent father, one who wants us to be happy, and who laughs at our foolish mistakes, never really taking things too seriously. He is our cosmic good buddy—our cheerleader. This image of God, although it contains some truth, is incomplete, and it can cause us not to go to confession because we simply don't take our sins very seriously.

So what does confession have to do with our friendship with Christ? One thing that's for sure—this sacrament is not about condemnation. Its purpose is to heal and reconcile our relationship with our truest, most faithful friend. This may not be the way it was presented to you in the past. If that's the case, you may have to let go of some preconceived notions of how God sees and relates to you. I know this isn't easy to do. It's hard to give things a second chance when they've caused us pain.

But Jesus tells us that we need to run to this sacrament in order to be healed. "Therefore, confess your sins to one another and pray for one another, that you may be healed. The fervent prayer of a righteous person is very powerful" (James 5:16). That being said, we usually don't run to this healing sacrament.

And here's why. I think there are a few things that scare all of us off from confession. First, I believe many of us are scared to talk to a priest about our sins. For many of us, the priest we end up going to confession with knows us and our families well. Awkward, right? But here's the thing: Priests hear so many confessions each and every week that they don't remember one from the next. One priest, Father Mike Schmitz, refers to this phenomenon as "divine amnesia." He claims that he hardly remembers anything he hears in confession. Isn't that amazing?

A beautiful saint named Faustina once heard these words of Jesus spoken to her heart: "My daughter, just as you prepare in My presence, so also you make your confession before Me. The person of the priest is, for Me, only a screen. Never analyze what sort of a priest it is that I am making use of; open your soul in confession as you would to Me, and I will fill it with My light."

How beautiful is that?

You see, the second part of being scared to talk to a priest about our sins is the reality that we aren't talking to a priest. Obviously there is a literal, physical priest you are talking to (I'm not crazy; I've seen him in the confessional, too), but the person you are *actually* talking to is Jesus. The priest is just standing in His place. So, the priest is there in body, but it is Jesus who hears your sins and forgives you of them, not the priest.

Sometimes, when I'm scared to talk to a certain priest when I go to confession, I close my eyes and imagine that I am just praying to Jesus. When you go to confession, try that. Close your eyes and imagine that you are face-to-face with Jesus in your heart. Then, say your sins to Jesus, not to the priest. And then, allow the forgiveness and love of God to wash over you.

Third, I think we don't love confession because we don't know what to say. It can be really hard to determine what is a sin and what is not. And sometimes we feel really awkward saying certain sins out loud.

I have heard some priests say it is best to just list your sins as briefly as possible and move on. Other priests prefer more detail and will ask you to flesh out your sins a little bit more. My best advice? Be bold in confessing your sins. Naming them out loud is important, so don't sugarcoat them. Bravely state the ways in which you have turned away from God, and allow yourself to be humbled by that.

As far as what is or is not a sin, this is where an examination of conscience comes in. Doing an examination of conscience will be very helpful in determining what you have done (or not done) that is a sin. And an examination of conscience is not just for you to use right before you go to confession; it can be done as often as every day.

To make it as simple as possible, a sin is anything that you have done to consciously turn away from the love of God. It is when you say to yourself, "I know that doing this [or not doing this] will not love God well, but I am going to do it anyway." Doing this separates you from God, and you must confess it in order to receive forgiveness and reenter into union with Him.

The good news? If you confess your sins, nothing can eternally separate you from God. His greatest desire is to forgive you and be with you.

Imagine it this way: God's hand is constantly reaching down to you. He wants to hold your hand more than anything. But when you sin, your grip on His hand loosens. Suddenly your hand will begin to slip until you are barely holding on to the tip of His finger. And as you add more sin, it will continue to loosen until you fall away from His hand altogether. But God's hand never moves. Even when you fall away from His grip, He is always reaching toward you. And when you go to confession, He beams and eagerly reaches down and accepts your hand back into His loving embrace.

It is comforting and safe to have someone holding your hand. And it's even better when that someone is Jesus.

This week, I encourage you to seek forgiveness in the sacrament of confession. Let Jesus love you. Respond to God's outstretched hand and allow Him to hold yours. Trust me, you will need His comforting grip as you walk through life. Hold on to this truth: Confession is about letting Jesus love you and responding to His love, and He always meets you with mercy.

Discussion Questions:

Do you prefer to go to a priest who knows you, or would you rather go to a stranger?

Do you find it hard to come up with things to confess?

Did anything I shared make you look at confession differently than before?

Quiet your heart. . . .

Ask your daughter for something specific that is on her heart—a dream, a worry, a troubled relationship—and pray for that desire or need.

Dear God,
Help us to see our lives and choices through Your eyes. Instead of justifying our sin, I pray we would take it seriously. But please, free our hearts from any fear that might rise up when we think about confessing our sins to You. Help us to remember that You always meet us with mercy and there is absolutely nothing that You won't forgive. But

keep us from believing the lie that says if we feel guilty, then the job is done. The guilty feeling needs to be followed with confession. May we take seriously the importance of confessing our sin, and be filled with gratitude for the fount of mercy that always meets us in the confessional.
Amen.

JOURNALING CONVERSATIONS

What circumstances make it easiest to have an honest conversation? When do you feel the most "heard"? Which is easier, talking face-to-face or journaling thoughts?

MOTHER

DAUGHTER

NOTES

Day 38

FORGIVENESS

Because we are God's beloved daughters, He wants us to grow in character and grace to our fullest potential. Wouldn't it be wonderful if we grew more like Jesus simply by experiencing only good things? If we are honest, we have to admit that we have grown the most through our struggles. The process may not have been pleasant, but the lessons learned were invaluable.

Think of three people in your life who consistently get a rise out of you—annoying you, making you angry, causing you to lose your patience. Do you know that they are some of the best tools in your life to make you more like Jesus?

When they say or do something that offends you or hurts you, you have a choice how you will respond. Author Ted Cunningham recommends, "when the emotion of anger arises within you, respond to God rather than react to people. What we mean by 'respond to God' is that you value all of the trials in your life."[33] You recognize that they bring you opportunities to grow in spiritual maturity and give you an opportunity to offer forgiveness.

Forgiving people who have hurt us can be extremely difficult, but because Jesus shows us mercy (in the sacrament of confession), we are called to show mercy to one another. In fact, He tells us in Scripture that we are called to "Be kind to one another, compassionate, forgiving one another as God has forgiven you in Christ" (Ephesians 4:32).

But what does it mean to forgive?

According to Saint John Paul II, "Forgiveness is above all a personal choice, a decision of the heart to go against the natural instinct to pay back evil with evil."

---

[33] Dr. Gary Smalley and Ted Cunningham, *From Anger to Intimacy: How Forgiveness Can Transform Your Marriage* (Ventura, CA: Regal, 2009), 42.

We often make forgiveness much more complicated than it needs to be. We believe this lie that if we forgive, we have to forget and be "OK."

More often than not, we base forgiveness on our feelings. We think that if we still feel mad or hurt, then we haven't truly forgiven the person. But the truth is, forgiveness is not about how we feel; it is about what we choose to do. It is simple. It is a decision of the heart.

We experience feelings of hurt for a reason. When someone hurts us, our feelings kick in to protect and guard our hearts against future hurt. So these lingering feelings of anger or hurt can actually be a good thing in the process of protecting yourself. That being said, they should not stop you from forgiving. Because forgiveness is something different.

Forgiveness is an action. It is a choice. It is something we do, not something we feel. It is a decision to choose to love the person who hurt us (even if we don't necessarily like them) instead of responding to them with hatred and evil. In other words, it is a choice to turn the other cheek, to be the bigger person, to not reciprocate the hurt we are feeling. And this can be extremely hard.

But here's an idea: Start with words. Tell the person who hurt you that you forgive them. Literally use the words "I forgive you." It's time we dumped the words "It's OK." Because the truth is, it's probably not OK. It is probably quite the opposite of OK. You see, saying you're OK implies that you are fine. And you don't have to be fine to forgive. You just have to be willing to choose to forgive.

"I forgive you."
"You are forgiven."

These are powerful words that can bring peace and healing. This is why when you go to confession, the priest ends with words of absolution, saying something along the lines of, "Your sins are forgiven." Imagine if the sacrament of reconciliation ended with the priest saying, "It's OK." How would you feel? Would you feel forgiven?

This is why when Jesus forgives people in the Bible He almost always uses the phrase "Your sins are forgiven." What a wonderful, intentional thing to hear! I imagine the recipient of this phrase always felt truly forgiven.

In order for us to truly forgive, we must use these intentional words of forgiveness rather than a lie that we are OK. These words will be healing for both the person we are forgiving and for us. They will be healing for us because they will trigger a healing process in our hearts so that our feelings of hurt will slowly dissipate. This may take days, weeks, months, or even years, but forgiving will be the only thing that will give our hearts the chance to eventually heal.

And, like in the sacrament of confession, in order to be forgiven, we must ask for forgiveness. We must go to the people we have hurt, say we are sorry, and ask them for forgiveness. This experience can be humbling and difficult, but the grace we'll receive is always worth it.

So today, I challenge you to forgive. I challenge you to use words of forgiveness to bless the people who come to you asking for grace. And I challenge you to ask for forgiveness. Ask people you have hurt for grace. Finally, I challenge you to choose to forgive despite lingering feelings of hurt or anger. In fact, I challenge you to pay attention to those feelings and reflect on them, asking God to go to those tender places in your heart and transform them with His love.

Discussion Questions:

Is there someone who has hurt you who you need to forgive?

Is there someone who you need to ask to forgive you?

Do you agree that there is a difference between saying, "It's OK," and saying, "I forgive you"? Why or why not?

Quiet your heart. . . .

Ask your daughter for something specific that is on her heart—a dream, a worry, a troubled relationship—and pray for that desire or need.

Dear God,
Sometimes we need to forgive, and other times, we need to be forgiven. It's always a temptation to ignore the hurt, to walk away, to distract ourselves so we don't have to deal with conflict. Give us the courage to go to tender places in our relationships and seek real reconciliation instead of covering things up. When our feelings don't match our words (words like "I forgive you"), we pray You would help us to stay strong with our decision to forgive, and then transform our feelings. May our hearts be full of gratitude for the countless times You have forgiven us. Because of all we have received from You, may our hearts overflow with forgiveness, love, and mercy.
Amen.

JOURNALING CONVERSATIONS

If you could live at any time in history, when would it be and what would you do?

MOTHER

DAUGHTER

Day 39

GOING THROUGH THE MOTIONS

Catholics often get a bad rap for simply "going through the motions" in their faith. People claim that Catholics don't really have a personal faith because all they have to do is show up to Mass on Sundays and pray the occasional Rosary. And you know what? That's true of a lot of Catholics. Instead of pursuing a personal relationship with Christ, they reduce everything to a checklist of spiritual rules that leave the head and the heart out of the picture.

A real relationship with Jesus requires humility and a willingness to wrestle with questions instead of giving up and walking away. Saint Teresa of Calcutta modeled this for us with her life. There were countless times when she couldn't make sense of the way God allowed her to feel. She experienced a great deal of darkness, and for much of the time, she had no explanation for why God didn't flood her with happiness in return for all she was doing for Him. She wrote, "If I ever become a saint—I will surely be one of darkness." She wrestled with her questions, never walked away, and continued to serve. The result? She changed the world. When things got hard, she stayed. She didn't give up.

As you grow older, you'll encounter more and more people who question why they need the Church. When Gen X Americans were asked by Barna Group[34] researchers about the importance of attending church, 49 percent said it is "somewhat" or "very" important, and 51 percent said it is "not too" or "not at all" important. The stats regarding millennials show that people are becoming less and less likely to be involved with the Church. Only two out of ten millennials think church attendance is important. There's no evidence of this trend shifting, which means most of your friends will likely walk away, and you might be tempted to do the same.

---

[34] The Barna Group, located in Ventura, CA, is widely considered to be a leading research organization focused on the intersection of faith and culture.

What has caused this change? At a time when women are outpacing men in college enrollment and completion,[35] many women are frustrated with what they perceive as a limited role within the Church. For some, the change is the result of a frustration with the way the Church relates to those experiencing same-sex attraction. Many cite hypocrisy within the Church as a prime reason for their disinterest. They are tired of people saying one thing and doing another. For others, this has gone a step further: They have been hurt by the Church and have walked away because of it.

Others feel that everything they hear in the Mass lacks relevance to the rest of their lives. They have limited time, and they'd rather spend it somewhere else. In addition, we are impacted by the consumerist mind-set of the Western world—we want what we want, when we want it, how we want it. We don't have patience with an experience that irritates us ("I can't stand the music"), bores us ("The homily was too long and had nothing to do with my life"), or offends us ("People here are out of touch with where people are at and are judgmental").

Maybe some of these thoughts have started creeping into your mind and heart. I wouldn't be surprised if they have. You are surrounded by a culture that tells you the Church is outdated and unnecessary. These messages are likely to have some influence in your life.

There's something important I want you to know: I am not afraid to hear about your questions and concerns. I cannot promise to have answers to all your questions, and I certainly can't defend or explain everything the Catholic Church does. But I am a safe place to come with your uncertainty. I would much rather hear where you honestly are in your faith than have you fake interest. I'm not saying it doesn't matter whether you go to Mass if you are struggling with your faith. What I am saying is that I don't want you to hide what you are struggling with. You can be respectful at Mass while dealing with questions. It's a matter of both/and.

All too often, when we start to question aspects of our faith, we open our ears wide to all who are ready to plant seeds of doubt, and we close the door on God's voice. How can God keep speaking to you if you don't ever open His love letter to you—the Bible—or you stop coming to Mass? Keep listening to Him during seasons when you struggle with your faith. Don't shut the door to Him and open another wide to the world. That will not lead you to peace or fuller understanding.

The frightening increase in suicide, anxiety, and depression among young people indicates that we do need truth we can stand on. What the world offers—what is

[35] Mark Hugo Lopez and Ana Gonzalez-Barrera, "Women's College Enrollment Gains Leave Men Behind," Pew Research Center, http://www.pewresearch.org/fact-tank/2014/03/06/womens-college-enrollment-gains-leave-men-behind/.

increasingly being consumed, embraced, and worshipped—is not leading people to a happier place.

When you come to restless periods in your life when you may be learning about many different philosophies and theological perspectives, you might find that all of them can be quite convincing. You can be easily tossed back and forth, depending on who makes the most sense at the time. This can rob you of inner peace and cause you to hit a wall in terms of spiritual growth. I don't want you to stay stuck in that place.

So when thoughts swirl and questions come, keep digging. Keep studying and don't stop talking about what you're thinking. At the same time, don't lose sight of the great gift you've been given in the Catholic Church. It can be an anchor for you in times of confusion and exploration.

A powerful video encouraging Catholics to "come home" says it well:

> Jesus, Himself, laid the foundation for our faith when He said to Peter, the first pope, "You are rock, and upon this rock I will build my church." For over 2,000 years, we have had an unbroken line of shepherds guiding the Catholic Church with love and truth, in a confusing and hurting world. And in this world filled with chaos, hardship and pain, it's comforting to know that some things remain consistent, true, and strong—our Catholic faith and the eternal love that God has for all creation.[36]

But there's an important quality that you'll need to hold on to if you are going to navigate questions and difficulties well: humility. In the words of Father John Bartunek:

> Being led by truth requires humility. It requires recognizing a higher authority than oneself: if I am obliged to discover, accept, and conform to what is objectively true (morally, physically, historically), then I am not autonomous; I am not the master of my universe; I am not God. That act of humility, which frees us from the enervating bonds of selfishness, is hard to make. Our fallen human nature tends toward pride, self-sufficiency, control, and dominance. To resist that tendency requires courage. It takes courage to obey the truth and expose oneself to the burning love of God.[37]

---

[36] Catholics Come Home, "2000 Years of Faith: The Truth Behind Our 'Epic' Evangomercial," http://www.catholicscomehome.org/wp-content/uploads/2012/12/CCH-Epic-Factual-Documentation-20121.pdf.
[37] John Bartunek, *The Better Part: A Christ-Centered Resource for Personal Prayer* (Hamden, CT: Circle Press, 2007), 977.

Staying humble, asking questions, digging for truth, and not being afraid of things that confuse you will set you up to experience a vibrant personal faith. I am here for you on your journey. Come to me with your questions and confusion. Together we can look for the answers. Just keep the door to God open and keep listening for His guiding voice. He isn't afraid of your questions. His love is greater than any uncertainty. He is the constant, the anchor, the truth you can hold on to.

Discussion Questions:

Which Church teachings confuse you?

Which Church teachings comfort you?

Are there times you are tempted to fake your faith?

Quiet your heart. . . .

Ask your daughter for something specific that is on her heart—a dream, a worry, a troubled relationship—and pray for that desire or need.

Dear God,
In Romans 1:25, Saint Paul said, "They exchanged the truth of God for a lie and revered and worshiped the creature rather than the creator." This exchanging of truth for a lie is so very subtle. It's a slippery slope—a gradual accepting of what the world says matters most. We don't worship creatures in the form of carved-stone idols, but we worship other things. And when we worship them by allowing them a place in our hearts that was meant for You alone, we start to believe all sorts of lies.

It takes a lot of humility and courage to ask, "God, where have I exchanged Your truth for a lie? Where am I defining the truth for myself instead of humbly accepting what You have said is right and wrong?" When we find a teaching of the Church that's hard to accept, help us to take some time to pray about it and study it with a humble heart. But thank You for being our safe place to explore—for allowing us to come to You with doubts and questions. You love us as we are, where we are. Always.
Amen.

JOURNALING CONVERSATIONS

My favorite thing to do with you is . . .

MOTHER

DAUGHTER

NOTES

Day 40

SET THE WORLD ON FIRE

God needs young women who are ready to set the world on fire. He is on the lookout for people who see the suffering, pain, and all that's not right in our world and choose to do something about it.

The more balanced you are in four key areas of life, the more effective you will be in bringing change and hope to the world. What does it look like to be a balanced person? This is someone who stands out in the crowd with a quiet confidence that comes from knowing how very much she is loved by her heavenly Father, and that He loves her not because of what she produces, but simply because she is His daughter and He is crazy about her. She knows where she is going and stays focused on what is most important, because her prayer life keeps her in constant contact with the Holy Spirit, who gives her all the guidance she needs. She's the best friend you can have, because of her gracious words, loyal heart, and consistent love. Though her circumstances may be difficult, she continues to walk with grace. Where does her strength come from? It comes from within, as God has transformed her heart to more clearly resemble His. This is a young woman God can use to do great things in our world!

A balanced young woman pays attention to four main areas of Christian living:

1. Spiritual life
2. Human development
3. Knowledge of the faith
4. Apostolic activity

Let's look at those four areas one by one. First of all, the **spiritual life**. In John 15:5, Jesus says, "I am the vine, you are the branches. Whoever remains in me and I in him will bear much fruit, because without me you can do nothing."

Nurturing and developing your spiritual life should be your highest priority. And what the spiritual life boils down to is establishing and maintaining an intimate friendship with Jesus Christ. Your prayer life is an excellent gauge for how that friendship is doing.

Just as your body needs food, your soul needs nourishment. God feeds our souls with grace through the Bible, the sacraments, and prayer. This takes time, and it must be given the highest priority in your life if you want to be a balanced young woman.

The second area is **human development**. This is the process of developing the basic character traits that should be seen in any person—not just a Christian. Speaking graciously, following through on your commitments, being a young woman of integrity (being the same person when no one is looking), having good manners, and taking care of yourself physically all are a part of human development. We also want to increasingly be women who are optimistic, who have an uplifting perspective on life. In a certain sense, your face doesn't belong to you. What do I mean by that? Think about how rarely you look at your face or see your own expressions. Those around you see these things far more often. Having a pleasant look on your face is a gift to others.

Colossians 3:12–15 sums up human development very well: "Put on then, as God's chosen ones, holy and beloved, heartfelt compassion, kindness, humility, gentleness, and patience, bearing with one another and forgiving one another . . . and over all these put on love . . . and let the peace of Christ control your hearts." To check yourself in this area, ask yourself, "Am I a person who I would want to be around?"

The third area is **knowledge of the faith**. This has to do with our intellectual development. The more we know about God and about our faith, the more we will love Him. The more we know what He expects of us, what the guidelines are that He has laid out for us in the Bible and in the teachings of the Church, the more we're going to make the right choices. Those right choices will correlate directly to our happiness. If we don't take the time to study our faith, we'll be blown around by whatever the current trends are in our culture, which may take us far from where God wants us to be. And being in the center of God's will is the safest and most satisfying place in the world.

Romans 12:2 calls us to give time to growing in knowledge of the faith: "Do not conform yourselves to this age but be transformed by the renewal of your mind, that you may discern what is the will of God, what is good and pleasing and perfect."

We need to pay attention to what we feed our minds. What are we watching on the screen? What are we reading? Are we filling our minds with truth? To check yourself in this area, ask yourself, "Do I know more about my faith this year than I did last year?"

The fourth area is **apostolic activity**. If we want to become more and more like Jesus, if He is our role model, then it's essential that we have a heart of service toward others. Mark 10:45 reminds us, "The Son of Man did not come to be served but to serve and to give his life as a ransom for many." It can be tempting to take all that God has given us and become very inwardly focused. Yes, our God is a personal God who loves each one of us individually, knows us intimately, and desires a relationship with us. But His intention is not for us to live in isolation. He wants us to take all that He gives us, all that He has developed in us, so we can better minister to a hurting world.

“Be who God meant you to be and you will set the world on fire!” –Saint Catherine of Siena

Discussion Questions:

In which area would you most like to grow: your spiritual life, human development, knowledge of the faith, or apostolic activity?

What did you think of the statement “In a sense, your face doesn’t belong to you”?

Do you think you know more about your faith this year than you did last year?

Quiet your heart. . . .

Ask your daughter for something specific that is on her heart—a dream, a worry, a troubled relationship—and pray for that desire or need.

Dear God,
Help our hearts to remain open to you, and give us the grace and desire to be continuous learners. In a spirit of humility, may we always endeavor to grow in closeness to you, in graciousness to others, in our knowledge of our faith, and in our willingness to serve others. May we do everything in your strength, through the Holy Spirit doing in and through us things that might otherwise be impossible.
Amen.

JOURNALING CONVERSATIONS

What is it like to experience you when you are overwhelmed or angry? What is it like being on the other side of you?

MOTHER

DAUGHTER

Appendix

NOTES

Appendix 1

SAINT TERESA OF CALCUTTA

PATRON SAINT OF BLAZE

Saint Teresa of Calcutta, more commonly known as Mother Teresa of Calcutta, was gifted with a heart to love the poorest of the poor. This blessed saint responded boldly to the call God had placed within her. She said yes to God with her whole heart, and because of her willingness to do so, she lived out her God-given purpose, became who she had been created to be, and set the world on fire. Saint Teresa is one of the greatest saints of our time because she was willing to turn away from the lie that the way she wanted to serve the people of Calcutta was impossible; instead, she wholeheartedly turned toward the truth that God would give her the strength to accomplish whatever He was calling her to do. When she turned to God and embraced this truth, her love was multiplied and the entire world was impacted by it.

BLAZE is intended to be a program that ignites the hearts of tween/teen girls and provides them with the tools they need to cast off the lies of the world and instead fix their eyes on the truth that Christ reveals. It endeavors to teach girls how to hear the call God is placing on their hearts, and it is meant to challenge them to respond to that call with boldness, love, and faith. It is our hope that the girls will recognize that despite their young age, they, too, can set the world on fire when they become who they are meant to be.

Sometimes we think that to be a saint we need to do something extraordinary, something superhuman, something miraculous. Saint Teresa of Calcutta proves that this is not the case. In fact, her call wasn't all that special. God didn't call her to end world hunger or eradicate all violence. He called her to do little things with great love. Her call was simply to love, right where she was. And that is exactly what she did. Mother Teresa humbly loved the poor of India with everything she had, and the ripples of her impact reached around the globe. God took one woman's brave yes and changed the world. BLAZE is intended to inspire girls to offer their own yes, right where they are planted. Just imagine what God can do through a generation of girls who know they are His beloved and bravely carry that message of hope to others.

Mother Teresa lived the gospel of love. In her own words, "We do not need to carry out grand things in order to show a great love for God and for our neighbor. It is the intensity of love we put into our gestures that makes them into something beautiful for God."[38]

Similarly, the challenges placed before girls in BLAZE are not huge. We are not asking them to give up everything they own for the poor or to run off and join a convent tomorrow. Instead, through this use of truths and lies, we are encouraging them to take a look at which lies have begun to take root in their hearts and to replace them with the life-giving truths of Jesus Christ. The changes are small, but when done with love, they can be astoundingly transformative.

Mother Teresa changed the world because she knew, deep in her soul, that her true identity was as a beloved daughter of God. She spent her life being filled up by divine love, and then allowing it to flow into the lives of others. Mother Teresa altered people's lives because she treated others like the beloved sons and daughters they were.

Our hope is that BLAZE will help girls begin to identify as the beloved and learn how they are called to love others like the beloved. We believe that if they do this, through the intercession of Saint Teresa of Calcutta, they, too, will set the world ablaze.

---

[38] Mother Teresa, *No Greater Love* (New York: MJF Books, 1997), 26.

NOTES

NOTES

"For to the one who has, more will be given"
Matthew 13:12

The Journey Doesn't End Here

~ Christ's Love Is Endless ~

Walking with Purpose is more than a Bible study—it's a supportive community of women seeking lasting transformation of the heart. And you are invited.

Walking with Purpose believes that change happens in the hearts of women—and, by extension, in their families and beyond—through Bible study and community. We welcome all women, irrespective of faith background, age, or marital status.

Connect with us online for regular inspiration and to join the conversation. There you'll find insightful blog posts, videos, and downloads.

For a daily dose of spiritual nourishment, join our community on Facebook, Twitter, Pinterest, Instagram, and YouTube.

And if you're so moved to start a Walking with Purpose study group at home or in your parish, take a look at our website for more information.

walkingwithpurpose.com

walking with purpose

NOTES

• Deepen Your Faith • Open Your Arms • Broaden Your Circle •

When your heart opens, and your love for Christ deepens, you may be moved to bring Walking with Purpose to your friends or parish. It's a rewarding experience for many women who, in doing so, learn to rely on God's grace while serving Him.

If leading a group seems like a leap of faith, consider that you already have all the skills you need to share the Lord's Word:

- Personal commitment to Christ
- Desire to share the love of Christ
- Belief in the power of authentic, transparent community

The Walking with Purpose community supports you with:

- Training
- Mentoring
- Bible study materials
- Promotional materials

Few things stretch and grow our faith like stepping out of our comfort zone and asking God to work through us. Say YES and soon you'll see the mysterious and unpredictable ways He works through imperfect women devoted to Him.

Remember that if you humbly offer Him what you can, He promises to do the rest.

"See to it that no one misses the grace of God" Hebrews 12:15

Learn more about bringing Walking with Purpose to your parish. Visit us at walkingwithpurpose.com

walking with purpose

NOTES

The guided tour of God's love begins here.

Opening Your Heart: The Starting Point begins a woman's exploration of her Catholic faith and enhances her relationship with Jesus Christ. This Bible study is designed to inspire thoughtful consideration of the fundamental questions of living a life in the Lord. More than anything, it's a weekly practice of opening your heart to the only One who can heal and transform lives.

Explore these topics and more:

- What is the role of the Holy Spirit in my life?
- What does the Eucharist have to do with my friendship with Christ?
- What are the limits of Christ's forgiveness?
- Why and how should I pray?
- What is the purpose of suffering?
- What challenges will I face in my efforts to follow Jesus more closely?
- How can fear be overcome?

A companion video series complements this journey with practical insights and spiritual support.

Opening Your Heart is a foundational 22-lesson Bible study that serves any woman who seeks to grow closer to God. It's an ideal starting point for women who are new to Walking with Purpose and those with prior practice in Bible study, too.

To share Walking with Purpose with the women in your parish, contact us at walkingwithpurpose.com/contact-us.

walkingwithpurpose.com

walking with purpose

NOTES

FEARLESS & FREE

EXPERIENCING HEALING AND WHOLENESS IN CHRIST

Fear is a powerful emotion, and part of the human condition. Life isn't easy. But we were never meant to go it alone. God has wired us for connection – to Him.

Do you long to be grounded in a love that will never fail you?

Fearless and Free is for any woman confronting the reality of her fears. When suffering slams into you and leaves you reeling, or you feel great one day, and down on the mat the next, turn to this Scripture study.

Do you long for healing and wholeness? Would you like to be grounded in a love that will never fail?

In these six compassionate lessons, you'll learn to:

- **WAKEN** to the reality of who you are in Christ,
- **WRESTLE** with the battle in your mind, and conquer the enemy who seeks to steal your true identity.
- Be strengthened as a **WARRIOR** to reclaim your footing and move forward in life.

Fearless and Free is not about surviving; it's about flourishing in Christ's love, the One who truly loves you completely and without end.

Learn more about *Fearless and Free* at walkingwithpurpose.com

walking with purpose

SO MUCH MORE THAN A BIBLE STUDY

NOTES

NOTES

Transformative Catholic Bible Studies

Walking with Purpose Bible studies are created to help women deepen their personal relationship with Christ. Each study includes many lessons that explore core themes and challenges of modern life through the ancient wisdom of the Bible and the Catholic Church.

Opening Your Heart

A thoughtful consideration of the fundamental questions of faith – from why and how to pray to the role of the Holy Spirit in our lives and the purpose of suffering.

Living In the Father's Love

Gain a deeper understanding of how God's unconditional love transforms your relationship with others, with yourself, and most dearly, with Him.

Keeping In Balance

Discover how the wisdom of the Old and New Testaments can help you live a blessed lifestyle of calm, health, and holiness.

Touching the Divine

These thoughtful lessons draw you closer to Jesus and deepen your faith, trust, and understanding of what it means to be God's beloved daughter.

Discovering Our Dignity

Modern-day insight directly from women of the Bible presented as a tender, honest, and loving conversation–woman to woman.

Beholding His Glory

Old Testament Scripture leads us directly to our Redeemer, Jesus Christ. Page after page, God's awe-inspiring majesty is a treasure to behold.

Beholding Your King

This study of King David and several Old Testament prophets offers a fresh perspective of how all Scripture points to the glorious coming of Christ.

Grounded In Hope

Anchor yourself in the truth found in the New Testament book of Hebrews, and gain practical insight to help you run your race with perseverance.

Fearless and Free

With an emphasis on healing and wholeness, this study provides a firm foundation to stand on, no matter what life throws our way.

Reclaiming Friendship

Let God reshape how you see and experience intentional relationships, deal with your past friendship wounds, and become a woman who is capable of the lifelong bond of true friendship.

Ordering Your Priorities

An immensely practical study that will help you put the most important things first. Discover not only what matters most in life, but also how to prioritize those things!

Choose your next Bible study at shop.walkingwithpurpose.com

walking with purpose

SO MUCH MORE THAN A BIBLE STUDY

Who We Are

Walking with Purpose is a ministry of Jesus Christ.

Why We Exist

Our purpose is to help women and girls know Jesus Christ personally by making Scripture and the teachings of the Catholic Church relevant and applicable.

Our Mission

Our mission is to help every Catholic woman and girl in America encounter Jesus Christ through our Bible studies.

Our Vision

Our vision for the future is that, as more Catholic women deepen their relationships with Jesus Christ, eternity-changing transformation will take place in their hearts – and, by extension – in their families, in their communities, and ultimately, in our nation.

walking with purpose

You can support our mission through a tax-deductible gift.
Learn more at walkingwithpurpose.com/donate